The Superstitions
and
Curious Beliefs
of
Old Sussex

GW00585183

W.H. Johnson

POMEGRANATE · PRESS

Front cover illustration: Dead Man's Hand (*see page 46*). [From a print
by Isaac Cruikshank, courtesy of the Neil. R. Storey Archive]

British Library Cataloguing-in-Publication Data.
A catalogue record for this book is available from the British Library.

ISBN 978-0-9559006-6-2

Published by Pomegranate Press, Dolphin House, 51 St Nicholas Lane,
Lewes, Sussex BN7 2JZ
pomegranatepress@aol.com
www:pomegranate-press.co.uk

Printed by 4edge, 7A Eldon Way, Hockley, Essex SS5 4AD

About the Author

WH Johnson is a former headmaster and schools inspector. Now retired, he lives in Eastbourne.

See his website: *www.johnniejohnson.co.uk*

Fiction:
The Macaroni Dancers and other stories
And Such Great Names as These (under the pseudonym Allen Makepeace)

Non-fiction:
Seaside Entertainment in Sussex
Sussex Disasters
Alfriston Past and Present
Alfriston Village School 1879 - 1908
Early Victorian Alfriston
Crime and Disorder in Late Georgian Alfriston
Previous Offences: Crime in 19th Century Sussex
Sussex Tales of Mystery and Murder
Sussex Villains
Sussex Murders
A Grim Almanac of Sussex
Surrey Murder Casebook
Surrey Tales of Murder and Mystery
Surrey Villains
Essex Villains
Essex Tales of Mystery and Murder
Kent Murder Casebook
Kent Tales of Mystery and Murder
Kent Stories of the Supernatural
A Grim Almanac of Kent
True Crimes from the Past: Kent

Acknowledgements

I am particularly grateful to:

Esme Evans, Honorary Librarian, Sussex Archaeological Society.

The following kind people who have helped me with information about fishermen's superstitions: Ann Foord, Michael Bignell, Colin Allchorn and Ted Hide of Eastbourne; Alan Hayes of Brighton; Paddy Boyle of Newhaven.

QueenSpark Books, Brighton, for permission to quote from *Catching Stories: Voices from the Brighton Fishing Community*.

Like many who write about Sussex I have drawn on the late and much lamented *Sussex County Magazine*.

I am especially indebted to the wonderful collections of superstitions by Opie & Tatem and Steve Roud and to the work of so many Sussex authors, especially the Victorians – William D Parish, vicar of Selmeston, John Coker Egerton, rector of Burwash, and Mark Antony Lower, antiquarian and historian. But most of all my gratitude and admiration go to Charlotte Latham, wife of the vicar of Fittleworth, whose collection of superstitions was made the hard way. Unlike me, she had little published work to consult. Instead she sought information from those around her – servants, labourers, shepherds, tanners, fishermen, farmers – any, in fact, who still recalled and indeed believed in the superstitions which had been part of the belief system for so many generations of Sussex folk.

As ever I am grateful to my wife, Anne, for her commentary on the manuscript and for proof-reading my initial error-laden script.

Every effort has been made to seek copyright permission. Any omissions of acknowledgement will be rectified in subsequent printings.

Contents

'Superstition is the poetry of life' – Goethe

'Superstition is to religion what astrology is to astronomy;
the mad daughter of a wise mother' – Voltaire

'I have, thanks to my travels, added to my stock all the
superstitions of other countries. I know them all now, and
in any critical moment of my life they all rise up in armed
legions, for or against me' – Sarah Bernhardt

'The worst superstition is to consider our own tolerable' –
Doris Lessing

*Ann Cruttenden, 'seduced by the instigation of the Devil', murdered her husband and was
burned at the stake at Horsham in 1776. [Courtesy of the Neil R. Storey Archive]*

Introduction

I can say quite briefly what decided me to write this book. In September 2008, in the space of a few days, two unrelated encounters got me thinking about superstition. First of all, a neighbour told me that he continued to buy lottery tickets every week without fail even though he had won only three very small prizes since the lottery began. He said, however, that he did not dare to stop buying his ticket because he knew that the very week he stopped his numbers would come up.

Then a day or two later, on a train journey, two young men came into the carriage and sat opposite me. I wasn't meaning to eavesdrop, but you know how compelling other people's conversations can be. They were talking football and one of them confessed that all season his favourite team – a Premiership side – had not lost whenever he wore a pair of red socks on a match day. He had worn them, he said, with his morning suit at his sister's recent Saturday afternoon wedding.

How illogical both of these seemed. My neighbour seemed to be telling me that the only way to avoid a misfortune was to keep on buying his lottery tickets: once he stopped doing so he would have to live for the rest of his days with heart-wrenching disappointment. This is a highly intelligent man telling me that the outcome of the lottery draw depended on his buying a ticket.

As for the young man in the train, he was as good as saying that the result of a football match depended absolutely on his wearing a particular pair of socks. Well, I know that since I overheard that conversation his favourite team has suffered some rather serious defeats. Has he now abandoned the socks? Have they been replaced by a new pair, perhaps of a different colour?

It was the sheer absurdity of these two instances that turned me to thinking more seriously about superstition. I remembered that my mother would not wear green; that my wife warns me not to tempt Providence when I express a too-optimistic expectation of some future event; that an uncle of mine, a mild, easy-going sort of man, put his foot down at the thought of anyone bringing white flowers into the house; that my maternal grandmother not only touched wood with some regularity but also blithely threw salt over her shoulder. Was she worried about the Devil? Was she trying to blind him? No, but lurking there with all of these people was some vague idea that they could prevent ill luck and even promote good fortune. Asked in the cold light of day about their ideas, perhaps all of them would accept their irrationality. But on second thoughts, perhaps not.

In any event my curiosity was roused, and I looked in the library for books about superstition. There were the quite wonderful modern reference books by Steve Roud and Opie & Tatem which cover all of the superstitions throughout the British Isles. I loved dipping into these but I came to realise that I should like to focus more closely on home. What had been written about Sussex superstitions? There certainly appeared to be no book devoted exclusively to this topic. But I kept plugging away. I turned to three much admired Sussex writers of the nineteenth century – Mark Antony Lower, John Coker Egerton and William Parish – and they all had something about superstitions in their books but unfortunately insufficient to satisfy my curiosity. Finally, by chance, I came across what I was looking for in the *Sussex Archaeological Collections*. At last, a book about Sussex superstitions. Charlotte Latham's work was a mine of fascinating material, but it was really confined to West Sussex. And it was published as a lengthy article in the first edition of the *Folklore Record* as long ago as 1878.

Having examined what was available, I decided to write this book, attempting to bring together from a range of sources the superstitions of the whole of Sussex. Nor was I deterred by Mrs Latham's rather testy description of superstitions as 'fictions implicitly accepted as facts on no ground whatever'. I do not intend to condemn those who held such quaint notions, those who believed in magic and charms, witchcraft and counter-spells. It does not matter what I, a twenty-first century man, think. What matters is how our forefathers saw their world. That is the purpose of what I have written. And let me warn the reader that for convenience I have referred throughout to 'the county'. No East and West Sussex for me. At least, not in this book.

Such a different world. For most Sussex folk it was a rural world, a very small-town world, a village-and-hamlet kind of world. People did not travel far, were for the most part illiterate, were unsophisticated. Their world view was formed by the communities they scarcely ever left. As William Parish, the vicar of Selmeston, wrote: 'The true Sussex man divides the world into two parts. Kent and Sussex form one division and all the rest is the sheeres [shires].'

There is the story, apocryphal but nevertheless in a real sense true, of the old chap from Heathfield who went up into 'the sheeres'. He stayed only a week. He couldn't abide it. 'Nothing to beat old England yet,' he announced on his return. 'No more furrin' parts for me.'

But what were our forefathers to make of the world in which they lived? How did it work? What was their place in it? It was within the narrow boundaries of the parish that such restricted views were formed, that the old tales were told, the bits of gossip rehashed, the history mangled. Here the explanations for what we today should see as perfectly normal happenings were interpreted in some inevitably unscientific way.

This world of the past was set with snares. How could men and women explain the accidents of death and illness which came out of the blue? For instance, in the night the pig lay on top of her farrow. Not one survivor. Not normal though, a thing like that, they might think. Must be some 'ill-wishing', some wicked spell, directed at the household and its members. What if the cow stopped milking or the stream ran dry? Was some malicious person 'overlooking' the animals? Were they victims of malevolent magic, of wicked spells and curses? And, if so, what could be done? One answer was to go the cunning-man. Tell him your troubles, your fears. Let him devise a counter-spell to release you and your household from whatever evil hung over it. When awful events occur you have somehow to defeat or propitiate whatever agent is responsible.

Supposing your child has a worrying ailment. Perhaps the charmer can help. His cure may involve baked mice. Or he may suggest using snake skin. He may propose some radical way of stopping bed-wetting. It all depends on the nature of the complaint.

And there are omens. They're enough to cause concern. You hear things, see things, and it is these which warn you of some dreadful event affecting you or your family or someone you know. The church bell sounds different today; a swarm of bees alights in a place different from usual; a door is left open after the corpse has left for burial. These are the signs. No doubt about it: another death will come along.

Here, in this atmosphere of irrational fear and apprehension, superstition thrives. Bad luck is always round the corner, disastrous outcomes can be expected. It's all part of life. Two nuns come along and the sight of them decides the fisherman that he will not risk going to sea today. But what is the connection here? Where is the logic? Another time and another place, and one night a farmer loses his temper with fairies when he finds them feeding his horses in his barn – and he does not live long after that. Just shows, you can't treat fairies so.

Of course, you can try to ensure you have good fortune; you can try to see into the future. There are ways if you know the right incantation and where and when to utter it.

In a churchyard a girl tries to conjure up the wraith of her future husband; her friend attempts to summon a wraith by sitting in the kitchen with her blouse drying by the fire. Both girls believe that what they are trying to do is possible. It is done all over the British Isles, this business of calling up the spectre of a living being. This is magic. This is dabbling in the occult.

This world is peopled with fairies and witches and the Devil. The behaviour of bees and birds and small animals warns of dark powers working against you. There were at one time tales of dragons and water serpents which could tear you and your home apart.

But from the seventeenth century there was a growing change of viewpoint on these matters. There came the Enlightenment, that great European intellectual movement, which set out to sweep away the clinging cobwebs of the past. Logic demanded such follies be consigned to an outer darkness where they rightly belonged. In 1736 government legislation in this country indicated that there was no longer such a crime as witchcraft. It was all old-fashioned nonsense. These notions were no more than old wives' tales. They were the stock-in-trade of downright frauds, out to gull the innocent.

But the ordinary man and woman, and especially those in rural areas, were impervious to such arguments. They held on to the old ideas. And along with the old ideas remained the old superstitions, the belief in magic, in powers of good and evil, quite beyond ordinary human understanding, proving that you cannot by law wipe out overnight the deeply held convictions of the past.

I hope that this account will show how superstitions and other curious beliefs continued in Sussex until the recent past, as they did elsewhere in the British Isles, and how they coloured the everyday world of our forefathers.

Witches

Right from the time of the emergence of organised society the witch played a central part. The most primitive tribes had – and still have – their shaman, half doctor, half priest, called upon to ensure their safety, to preserve them from wicked spirits, to help them through intercession with the spirit world with good hunting, good crop growing, good herding.

Later, more sophisticated societies had their doctor-priests, their astrologers, their interpreters of omens, many of them regarded as being capable of influencing events by magical means. All are found in the great pre-Christian civilisations of Mesopotamia: the Sumerians, the Babylonians, the Assyrians. Later, in Greece and Rome, both highly developed societies with many gods, the seers and augurs sought for signs in a variety of sources such as animal entrails and the movement of birds. These priestly figures formed a bridge between everyday reality and the spiritual dimension.

In Europe, throughout the Middle Ages and later, monarchs and those holding the most influential positions in the land employed practitioners of the magic arts to recommend by one or other means the best courses of personal and political action. The scholar John Dee, alchemist, mathematician, astrologer, cast the future Queen Elizabeth's horoscope. The storms which later destroyed the Spanish Armada were raised, so it was said, by a spell cast by Dee. Not that all those engaged in the occult arts were seen as benevolent. At a time when demonic power was universally recognised, some unfortunates were charged with being agents of the Devil. Among the several charges laid against Elizabeth's mother, Queen Anne (Boleyn), by Henry VIII and the churchmen who advised him, were accusations of sorcery and bewitchment, the means by which she was said to have ensnared the king.

In this book, for convenience, the term generally used for such people will be 'witch', in Sussex encompassing both male and female practitioners of magic. It was quite usual for ordinary people to consult local witches, seeking advice on matters which concerned them: health, marriage prospects, minor financial investments, land purchases. But for centuries, the genuine and desperate fear of some witches, their powers thought to have been given them by the Devil, cast a permanent shadow across whole communities. There were times when, throughout the country, witches were accused of acting in concert with the Devil and they were tried and, if found guilty, hanged.

It is with these witches accused of wicked acts that this chapter deals – with the reminder that many, particularly women, were very frequently falsely accused.

Remarkably enough, and despite the frequency of witch trials at different periods, few were ever held in Sussex, and even then only one of the accused is known to have been put to death. This took place in 1575 when Margaret Cooper of Kirdford was found guilty of bewitching Henry Stoner on 1 April 'who languished until 20th April following, when he died'. There were two other charges brought against Margaret, these relating to the deaths of William Fowler in 1572 and Elizabeth Fowler in 1574. Were these poisoning cases? Margaret's husband was described as 'a surgeon'. Does that really mean that he was a cunning-man and that, if so, she had been just been prescribing some ineffective folk-cure used by her husband? Was the problem only that the cure did not work? Perhaps Margaret Cooper was simply unfortunate.

At the East Grinstead Assizes in 1591 Agnes Mowser from Fletching was found guilty of bewitching the late Ann Flemens. Agnes was given only one year's imprisonment, a sentence which usually carried with it four six-hour sessions in the pillory. Considering the charge, this does seem a light sentence. Does it suggest that the jury was not completely convinced that Ann Flemens' death was the result of witchcraft?

In 1572 at East Grinstead, Joan Usbarne of Hailsham, was found guilty of bewitching to death John Browne's bull valued at 40 shillings. She was sentenced to one year in prison with, of course, the accompanying pillory punishments.

At Horsham Assizes in 1577, Alice Casselowe of Mayfield faced two charges of bewitching to death an ox belonging to Magin Fowle and two pigs, the property of Richard Roose. She was sentenced to one year in prison where she died. Perhaps the pillory proved too much for her.

Then in 1607 came the protracted trial at Rye in which two women, Susan Swapper and Ann Taylor, were accused of 'conversinge with spirittes' – in other words, of witchcraft. If the evidence presented at other trials was as garbled as it was at this one, it is unsurprising that a jury of aldermen eventually dismissed the charges.

Rye is interesting, for there were twice as many accusations of witchcraft here as in all other Sussex towns and villages combined. Here, in 1610, Joan Bayly, aged 'four score years and upwards', became convinced that the child of a local fisherman, Thomas Hart, was bewitched. She told his wife, Susan, to bring her 'a piece of red cloth, three score needles and a half pennyworth of pins and by God's help she would cure the child'. She stuck the needles and pins in the cloth, put the bundle on the fire and then thrust a dagger into it. The next person to enter the house, she said, would be the one who had bewitched the child. In this case, the spell seems not to have worked.

Drawing again from the rich documentation of the Corporation of Rye, we meet the widow Anne Hownsell in 1645, accused of making nocturnal visits to the home of William and Frances Royall. On one occasion she appeared in Mrs Royall's bedroom without opening the door and another time she arrived through an upper storey window and left the same way.

Mrs Hownsell was examined physically and a red mark, commonly thought to be the sign of a witch, was found on her breast, the spot at which her satanic familiar, a dog, was said to suck the blood which sustained it. The mayor ordered her and another woman 'to be tried by putting them into the water'. There is no indication about whether or not either woman floated but at Rye Sessions in November 1645 both were found guilty of an unnamed felony and sentenced to be hanged, though there is no record of this sentence being carried out.

This was during that brief period when the monstrous witch hunts conducted by Matthew Hopkins and John Stearne, slap-bang in the middle of disorders of the Civil War, led to 250 people being charged with witchcraft. Of these at least a hundred hanged, but Sussex seems to have been relatively untouched by the furore, though the resonance of trials elsewhere, with their recitals of the wickedness of some witches, must have caused many a shudder.

At Horsham in 1654 Jane Shoubridge of Withyham was accused of employing 'certain wicked and divellish arts called witchcraft, inchauntments, charmes and sorceryes in and uppon one Mary Muddle of the age of twelve years', whose body 'was greatly wasted consumed pyned and lame'. In the indictment she was accused of being 'a common witch and enchauntress, moved and seduced by the instigation of the Divell'. Along with Clement

Shoubridge, Jane was held responsible for the deaths of two other children, but both accused were acquitted on all charges.

Another defendant, Alice Nash, was accused of bewitching two-year-old Elizabeth Slater and her sister, the five-year-old Anne, both of whom had died. But Alice also was acquitted. No matter how convinced the majority of jurymen must have been that witches existed, they were not in this case swayed by the accusations of the parents.

Times were changing. No longer were the old ideas accepted so readily. By the late 1600s, the time of the burgeoning Enlightenment, the Age of Reason, many in Europe were questioning the old certainties, untying the suffocating bindings of medieval thought. Now the cloying beliefs of past ages were increasingly subjected to rigid, scientific investigation and logical argument.

Did working out the future by interpreting images seen on the surface of a bowl of boiling oil or in a crystal or before a mirror seem reasonable? Could the spirit of a dead person be conjured up and spoken to? Could the direction of a flight of birds really give some kind of warning? Could a bullock's liver be relied upon to give advice on the next move in life? All of these sorts of questions were now being raised among the educated minority, and the conclusion increasingly accepted was that reliance on witchcraft was totally unreasonable, that it was a fraudulent absurdity. But it was only after years of agonising and wrangling that the matter was finally resolved, at least to the satisfaction of the law makers.

In 1736, parliament decided in the name of justice and reason that witchcraft was no longer a criminal act. The whole business of casting spells on people and their property was just so much mumbo-jumbo which had been believed in down the centuries. Now the philosophers, the politicians and the scholars had concluded that it was time to rid the world of such fatuous delusions. Reason now dictated that the whole business of claiming to foresee the future by casting spells and making magic cures was nothing but plain ignorance. And 'ill-wishing', so that a man's pig or, worse, his wife and children, went into a decline was just so much medieval twaddle.

Enough of it, then. From now on there was to be no more dragging suspected witches to the horse-pond, no more tying left hand to right foot, right hand to left foot, before throwing them into the water to test whether they floated or sank. Such crudities as 'swimming' were no longer to be tolerated. In future no-one would be weighed against the Holy Bible to seek out those who were unnaturally light, so light that they weighed less than the good book, so light that it was clear to all that they possessed dark and fearful powers. And any attempt to stick pins in anyone under suspicion or to scratch them with scissors or using any other method to make their blood flow, simply to ascertain how they responded, was to be treated as assault. From now on our legislators determined that the struggle would not be against the wickedness of witchcraft: now it was the superstitious follies of the uneducated masses that were to be countered. After all, look at these so-called witches, mostly poverty stricken women. How could such miserable creatures be in league with the Devil, such feeble souls deny God's own powers?

The Act was designed for the protection of those 'ignorant persons [who] are frequently deluded and defrauded' and the punishment of all who claimed 'to exercise or use any kind of witchcraft, sorcery, enchantment, or conjuration, or undertake to sell fortunes'. Such offenders could face a year in prison without bail and be made to stand in the pillory four times in the year. A better option than a hanging, perhaps, although from time to time even a single hour in the pillory could prove fatal.

When Mother Marjorie was turned out of the recently built alms houses at Rye, she was accused of practices 'such as any Christian heart would abhor to hear spoke of much less to be used'. When the alms houses were searched, pieces of raw beef, decaying, were found. It was thought that as the meat decayed, so would the bodies of those she had cursed. Already, so it was said, a man had hanged himself because of her spells. But the times had changed. Mother Marjorie was not brought before any court. Instead she was ejected from the town. Years earlier she might have faced the death penalty. We are unaware how her new neighbours were to regard her.

Now the legislation was on the look-out for those out to gull the innocent. A laudable enough aim, save that the innocents were unconvinced. The notions of the Age of Reason didn't reach down as far as the lower orders. All right for the sophisticated, the educated, the grand metropolitans, to come forward with such fine ideas but the fact was that for the most part everyone else knew that there were folk endowed with a different kind of knowledge. And this conviction of the power of magic, the existence of witchcraft and its accompanying fears, were not easily banished from the public mind.

Two hundred years later, despite the legislation, people in Sussex were still convinced of the existence of witches. In the early 1930s an 80 year old

Sussex countryman, told that there were no witches, that the whole idea of there being such people was rubbish, burst out, 'All rubbish? It ain't! Why, I knew a witch myself in this very village. Her daughter's alive still.'

And many others were in no doubt about what went on in these cottages inhabited by those they regarded as witches. They made bees-wax models of their intended victims and put them on the fire or they beat the model with a stick. That's what they did. Everybody knew that. And the consequences? The victim suffered terribly, their bodies painful and sometimes bruised. Or the witches could bring the rural economy to a halt: they could stop horses ploughing or they could misdirect reapers and even completely delay harvesting. True? Course it was. What did those people making laws up in London know about these things?

In the 1940s the *Sussex County Magazine* carried several accounts of witches who had been alive within living memory. One old man referred to a witch who had died shortly before. He was concerned that there had been a witches' book in the house. Presumably he thought it carried spells capable of raising the Devil, destroying whole flocks of sheep, laying waste to the land. Fortunately 'one of her daughters took it out of the village and a good thing too. We don't want any truck with that kind of thing'. Doubtless locals had been aware of the witch's potent force before her death, but no-one had done anything about it. Perhaps they were afraid of the consequences if they tried to do anything.

In 1943 a correspondent to the same magazine described a witch who had been alive only twenty years earlier. Because her daughter was still alive the witch was given the pseudonym, Betsey Shadlow.

'That kind of wicked old woman always has books - powerful books, which have a deal of evil written in them. I know Betsey had books because I've seen them. She was a very old woman at the time I'm telling you of, and when her husband – a quiet, ordinary chap – died, she found it hard to carry on as she'd been used to. For one thing, money was short, and for another thing her wickedness was rewarded with chronic rheumatics. She went on as best she could, but it was not easy, as no-one would lend her a hand, being frightened of what she might do to them. She used to swear away to herself when she lifted potatoes from the garden, and made a great trouble of going to the farm for milk. I remember the farmer wouldn't let her pass the gate for fear she would put a spell on the cows. She had to get on the road side of the gate and holler out. The farmer's wife were a bit hard of hearing, and many's the time old Betsey stood there and bawled her head off for half an hour at a time. Then her rheumaticky hands made it hard for her to do a bit of washing on a Monday morning.

'Gradually she dropped off coming into the village for provisions, making one visit do a long time, until one day the farmer said in the Woodman's Arms that old Betsey must be drinking ale, as she hadn't been near him for milk for quite a week. Well, to cut a long story short, the keeper did tell the rector, who called at the old woman's cottage that afternoon to find her ill in bed, hardly able to move a finger.

'The workhouse people came next day and took her away. One of the headmen stayed behind to sort out her belongings. She hadn't much furniture, but they found a pile of books. My neighbour, who was very fond of reading and very curious as well, asked the official if he could have them, or at least read them, but we said it wasn't right, and anyway we didn't want anyone else learning the secrets and playing us up – Betsey Shadlow was trouble enough – and we asked the workhouse chap to burn them. He looked at them and said they were rubbish anyway.

'It's a strange thing, but when they came to set fire to all the unwanted stuff from the cottage along with those books, we lookers-on saw green flames coming from the fire!'

Yes, and in some societies any kind of book is suspect.

At one time all classes had believed in witchcraft and all, high and low, had shared a fear of the occult powers at the disposal of witches. Now the educated, heirs to the Enlightenment, had rejected the outworn notions of so many past centuries. But broadly speaking, the poor, the barely literate, stuck in the world of a long-gone past, retained the old beliefs. And so the stories surrounding local witches, their powers for good and evil, continued to be told, becoming ever more fantastic in the telling, landmarks of the oral tradition.

Witches' familiars, it was well known, were generally handed down on a witch's deathbed to a successor. Had not every witch her familiar, her imp, in which her malignant power resided? And were not these familiars in the form of some small animal? Wasn't there always a cat or a dog, a mouse or a toad, present?

There are constant references to witches sitting comfortably in the shadows of the room, nursing the dog, stroking the mouse, suckling the toad.

 And sometimes it was believed that the evil resided outside the cottage, within a turkey cock or a chicken. You only had look in some old crone's cottage or outside in her garden, and there was the familiar, always with something about it that was different from the ordinary, a cat that was more than a cat, a dog more than a dog. Enough to make the blood run cold, the very sight, the very thought of them.

In the 1860s, when Dame Killick of Crowborough, worn out by the years, lay dying in agony, her daughter would not remain in the room with her, preferring to spend time in the garden. Was there some reluctance to accept what she knew was to be her inheritance? Upstairs, the old lady struggled with the familiar's spirit inside her, hoping for release from her wearisome burden, while the nurse urged the daughter to come to her mother's bedside. Would she not come to release her mother from her agonies? Eventually after much persuasion, the daughter did as requested and the spirit was immediately released to take up its new abode.

In the late nineteenth century when Old Mother Venus, attended by some local women, was dying, she sat up suddenly, 'cast her eyes quickly over the group of women standing near, and swiftly passed her hand to the breast of Mabel Ockley. Then Mother Venus fell back dead! "What did she give you?"questioned the women. "She gave me nothing," was the reply. But the witchcraft had been passed on.'

In 1933 Tom Reed, whose mother was one of those present at the deathbed, said that he believed that, just before the old lady passed away, Mabel had been given a mouse. Not that she was a very happy recipient. At least not according to the story which tells that her cottage was shortly afterwards subject to poltergeist activity as a result of which she upped sticks and left for Kent.

So what were these powers that were handed on? Well, it was said that witches could pass through keyholes, move stealthily up and down chimneys so that they could learn the secrets of every household. And they were guilty of the most awful crimes, casting spells on people and their families and their homes. That was power enough. But two of those most commonly spoken of powers related to the abilities of witches to turn themselves into animals and to immobilise wagons. Time and time again these stories crop up. Take the shape-shifting, the expectation that a human with special powers could change into an animal. There were references to this as far back as the twelfth century and it was mentioned frequently by witnesses in post-1736 court cases. The hare was a great favourite of the witches. In the form of hares it was thought they sucked cows' udders in the night, leaving them dry for the morning's milking.

Sometimes they were held responsible for damage to crops. For instance, take this account from a farm labourer, the author trying to capture the typical speech of Sussex men well over a hundred years ago:

'My mates and me was resting under a hedge nigh Up Waltham, 'aving our dinner, when a hare comes lopping along. Darky Tussler says, "That bain't a hare, that's that – ol' 'ooman down along under", (speaking of a village where we was lodging). I takes up a stone and throws it, and catches that hare. She didn't half holler, letting out a screech just like an ol' 'ooman, an' then she goes limping away. That night, when we was down in the village, ol' Sary Weaver, wot people said could make a cow run dry by lookin' at her – folks said she were a witch – comes 'obbling outer 'er cottage. When she sees we, she lets out a screech, same as the hare did, and goes a-limping off, for all of the world as if she were that there hare. She were lame in the same leg wot the hare was, but she 'adn't been afore!'

Note the line 'folks said she were a witch'. What do you make of that? It seems to suggest that Sary Weaver was suspected of being a witch but that there was no proof of her guilt. Presumably no-one in the locality was taking any action against her.

Dame Garson of Duddleswell was another of those able to shape-shift. Word had it that this was the way she could find out what she wanted to know about people especially those she intended to harm. One day, in hare guise, she was chased by huntsmen but managed to jump over into her garden and through one of the windows and into the house. Then those peering over the garden hedge heard a triumphant voice from inside calling out: 'Ah, my boys, you ain't got me yet.'

Boys Firmin, writing in the 1890s, says that the man who told him this story claimed to be present on that occasion. 'It's no use telling what's not true. Why, I be there myself and see it. It's quite true,' he told Firmin. 'The hare was Dame Garson herself.'

Another witness, an old man in West Sussex, claimed to have seen a woman known to be a witch walking by a hedge: 'I says, why, missus, you ain't no call to be out so late as this! And I tell you, as true as I'm sitting here, she vanished, and instead of her I saw a hare running through a gap in the hedge. I saw it – and you could have knocked me down with a feather.'

In the last years of the nineteenth century, Old Nellie, who lived in a hovel at Crossbush near Arundel, was crippled for life after someone had shot her mistaking her for a hare.

Old Mother Digby who lived in Hog's Lane in East Harting was another who changed into a hare though she went out attended by her own dogs – her familiars perhaps. Squire Russell of Tye Oak chanced upon her several times but never managed to catch her though on one occasion, just by her cottage, one of his dogs managed to bite the hare's behind, but then the fleeing animal slipped away down a drain. When the squire burst into the cottage, there was Old Mother Digby in human form. There was no sign of any hare. But the squire did notice that she was rubbing her behind.

Again according to Tom Reed, a friend of his, a man by the name of Crowhurst, caught an animal one night in the garden of a house said to be haunted by a witch. There was a struggle, Crowhurst hanging on to the animal for all his worth. He shouted for his companion to bring him the light so that he could see what it was he was wrestling with but when the light shone on his hands, they were empty. Impossible to catch a witch, Tom said. He was quite convinced of that.

Another time – and this is a creepy kind of tale – Crowhurst said that he had shot a cat in the leg because whenever his wife was out it used to come into his garden: his wife came home from market shortly after this and she was limping. She told her husband that she had fallen down. Poor Crowhurst. Was this another example of a shape-changing witch being injured in her guise of an animal?

This hare-sighting has the feel of a rural myth about it. It crops up so frequently and well beyond the boundaries of Sussex. In fact it is told across the British Isles and similar tales of wounded hares and injured witches are common. Charlotte Latham, wife of the vicar of Fittleworth, writing in the 1870s, said: 'I have met with even educated persons who, if a hare were the first animal that crossed their path upon their leaving home, would turn back, regarding it as a warning.'

Another witch-wounding story involves Dame Neve, who lived in the Crowborough area. For some reason or other, she had a grudge against a woman living in a cottage near Two Chimneys Chapel and she one day cast a spell which made it impossible for the woman to make butter. It must have been frustrating to find herself in the dairy but having no success, no matter how much she churned and churned. No doubt she whispered the charm she used when the butter-making was slow, confident that the actions of any witch would be nullified and additional help would come from good fairies. It usually did the trick.

But this time the cream in the churn was stubborn. When the woman's son came home he told his mother to leave the dairy. He would take over. The butter would come soon enough, he told her. But it did not. The son had no more success than his mother even though he used the charm as well. There was now only one solution as far as he was concerned. He took the poker and stuck it in the fire until the tip was red-hot and then he thrust it into the churn. There was a hissing sound almost like a scream after which the cream turned easily into butter.

The young man made his way back to work without telling his mother about how he had made the butter come. On the road he met Dame Neve hobbling along. 'Oh, my boy, give me something to put on my leg,' she implored him, 'for it is terribly burnt,' but he ignored her. The irony of this tale is that the witch went to the very cottage, begging help from the woman on whose butter-making she had so recently cast a spell. Unaware that she had been a victim of witchcraft, the woman kindly gave her some lard and a bandage to put on her injury.

Just to pause the narrative for a moment: these witches were greatly feared and were supposed to have great powers but they so often seem to have involved themselves in mean, rather cheap tricks. After all, if you can cast powerful spells, why simply stoop to interfering with churning butter? Or did some spiteful women at times insinuate their way into the milking parlour and surreptitiously drop a small slice of soap in the churn? That did the trick on more than one occasion. No witchcraft there.

The other frequently told story is of witches bringing farm carts to a halt. Again, if witches did have such abilities, it does seem a gross misuse of their powers, messing about with such low-level pranks. Here they are then, these witches, allegedly possessed of considerable occult powers but spending their time stopping kettles from boiling, interfering with the churning, causing loads of hay to fall off wagons and into quagmires and sending swarms of bees to attack those they did not like. And you begin to wonder if sometimes people were blamed for what were simply natural accidents. Was every pig, every child, every labouring man who fell sick, the victim of a spiteful witch?

At Ditchling, a witch living at the aptly named Jack o' Spades cottage was said to bring carts to a halt at her front door with some regularity, and that apparently, unlike most witches, she seemed not to have hidden her glee at her petty successes.

A witness said of these occasions: 'The men 'ud beat the hosses, an' they'd pull an' they'd tug, but the wagon wouldn't move, an' the ol' witch 'ud come out a-laughin' an' a-jeerin' at 'em, an' they couldn't get on till she let 'em. But there wor a carter wot knew, an' he guessed he'd be even wid the ol' witch, so he druv his wagon before her door an' then it stopped, an' the hosses they tugged an' they pulled, and they couldn't move it nohow an' he heard this ol' witch a-laughin' in the cottage. Then this carter wot knew, he took out a large knife an' he cuts notches on the spokes, an' there wor a screeching an' a hollerin' inside, an' out come the old witch a-yellin' an' sloppin' blood, an' for every notch on the spokes there wor a cut on her finger.'

Iron was the answer, for witches had no answer to its mighty power. Presumably it stopped the Ditchling witch, and the same remedy seems to have worked elsewhere. H.S. Toms, the curator of Brighton museum in the

1920s, heard a similar story: 'I was told at Findon of a witch who resided, not within living memory, in a cottage by the Sussex Pad, near Old Shoreham Bridge; and that when carters passed that way, they were in the habit of running the blade of their pocket-knife round the iron tyres of their wagon wheels. By some mysterious means, this so affected the witch in her cottage that she was heard to cry aloud in agony.'

There was a similar tale about a witch at Plumpton and about another rejoicing in the name Dame Prettylegs who lived at Albourne. Yet another witch, living at Stedham, once halted a carter's wagon and then apparently relented and showed him how he might break the spell by flogging the wheel with his whip. But there is no record of her having given up her wicked ways permanently.

On another occasion on the road from Middleton to Slindon two horses pulling a wagon laden with wood came to a sudden halt. The carters were unable to move the shivering, sweating beasts until they hit on the idea of taking a heavy chain off the wagon and dragging it along the road. Immediately the spell was broken and the horses recovered at once.

It does seem that these accounts, firmly believed by so many at the time, have the quality of fairy stories. There are the repetitive themes leading frequently to the eventual outwitting of the witch.

In Hurstpierpoint in 1895 there were still some memories of Nanny Smart who had lived in the village a hundred years before. It was said that so great was the fear she aroused that she could enter any house she pleased and demand tea. And she could put people in a trance, could make them as immobile as she made horses. Furthermore, like all witches, she could not die until she found someone to accept her power. She was said to have sold her secrets to a Cuckfield man called Hockland who bought them for a ha'penny and she straightaway afterwards died in a blue flame. As for Hockland, despite his newly inherited power, he ended his days in the workhouse, just as impoverished as many another old witch,

The ability to put people into a trance crops up in a number of cases. A farmer in Climping who frequently spied on his labourers from the top of a hayrick fell foul of one of his employees who just happened to be a witch. The story goes that on one occasion the farmer was transfixed and unable to move from his hayrick for two days. Near Chichester a woman always referred to locally as 'the Witch' was blamed for every misfortune, her victims describing themselves not as 'bewitched' but as 'sin-struck.' A groom working at West Dean told his master that there was no resisting her power: 'If she willed that I should sit across the roof of this stable from morning to night she'd have me up there in an instant, and nothing could bring me down till she gave me leave to come.'

At Mark Cross, farmer Pigtail Bridger, so called because of the antiquated hair style he adopted, was thought to have occult powers. He was, witnesses said, 'a very tall, big man, terrible to look at.' We are to assume that this referred to his physical appearance though his dress sense might also have contributed to the description. Whilst the chocolate-coloured neckerchief he wore might not have seemed out of the ordinary, the rest of his costume was unusual. He wore 'gussikins', short trousers reaching just below the knee, no socks or stockings and on his feet he had loose slippers. Not the most suitable working dress for farm work.

But Pigtail was possessed of an amazing power and was capable of casting a spell over anyone, able to reduce anyone to total helplessness. Until he was released, the victim remained in whatever position he was in at the time the spell was cast. If his workers, who unsurprisingly were terrified of him, slacked or complained, this was the way he would punish them. And it was no good the men muttering quietly among themselves, for Pigtail – so it was said – could read their thoughts. And so, just at dinner time, when they came in to eat round the farmhouse table, he would transfix whoever had fallen short, leaving him within inches of his broth or suet pudding or cheese and bread. Now the poor soul would be taunted. Why so slow in setting about his dinner? Why continue to stand when there was a place on the bench for him? Had he lost his appetite? Come on, man. Sit down and set to. But there were those who said that Pigtail was in reality a generous soul, given to playing no more than parlour tricks. But were they magical tricks? Or did he have the hypnotic powers similar to modern day stage performers of magic?

And then there was the case of the eminently respectable member of the gentry up to similar tricks. In 1872 Mr M.W. Harrison wrote to the then rector of Hartfield asking about a relative who had died in the previous century. He was inquiring about Timothy Luff of Kent House at Harting in West Sussex. He was sure that his relative could cast horoscopes and imagined that he was able to hypnotise people, having what Mr Harrison described as 'Mesmeric Power'. He was of the view that not only was Mr Luff 'a Gentleman and a Great Lover of the More Natural Sciences', but regarded 'by his Poorer Neighbours as a Wizard or Sorcerer'. Mr Harrison had been given to understand that he 'could transfix immovable a Waggoner, Waggon, and 4 Horses'. In his letter Mr Harrison gives the impression that he believes his relative to be principally an enthusiastic if amateur scientist. What he is describing, however,  is a man with magical powers using them simply to play little more than pranks. Were the locals simply mistaken in thinking that a man interested in such matters must have sold his soul to the Devil?

And it was certainly believed that some people had sold their souls to the Devil. Wasn't it a well-known fact? Hadn't a fisherman in Hastings done that? There was no doubt about it. Other crew members knew it. 'It was currently reported that he could creep through a keyhole and he had made a witch of his daughter in order that he might have the more power over his fellows. It was also believed that he could sit on the points of pins and needles. His brother fishermen put it to the test whenever they had the opportunity. In the alehouses he frequented they often placed long needles in the cushions of the chairs in such a manner he could not fail to pierce himself when he sat down. The result of these experiments tended to confirm their faith in his supernatural powers. It was asserted that he never flinched.'

Witchcraft might have been dismissed in the legislation of 1736 but it did not dispel a general belief in it for another couple of centuries. In a letter to *The Times* a contributor recollected that in about 1900 an old Sussex woman had told her 'the day, hour, and place where, if I went, I could watch all the local witches meet and career on their broomsticks. It was midnight, in early January, and on an exposed space on Burwash Ridge.'

This correspondent to *The Times* was really concerned to point out that such outlandish notions were still accepted by some Sussex folk.

There is little doubt that down the ages countless innocent men and women were falsely accused of being witches. In 1842 the wife of a labourer who lived on New Pound Common at Wisborough Green had been ill for a considerable time and could not understand why her illness was so protracted. She had talked matters over with her neighbours and they had concluded that she was bewitched. They suspected that the witch was another local woman, described as 'a very decent, inoffensive creature' but appearances can deceive. The sick woman along with her neighbours tried a number of strategems to destroy the witch's power but all of these failed. Finally they somehow hit upon a scheme which they hoped might work. *The Sussex Agricultural Express* reported: 'They procured pigeons and tied them in pairs back to back by their wings and lighted a large fire, and stopped up [sealed] the room as close as possible; some of the poor pigeons they opened at the breast in order that the fire might burn their hearts while alive. How many were burned, the writer cannot say, but he heard a neighbour state that he himself had burned four, and he thought they should have destroyed the witch if the house had been

 closer [more tightly sealed]. It is supposed by the neighbours that a dozen to sixteen pigeons were destroyed in this cruel manner.'

As tradition demanded when counter-spells were used, during the whole hideous operation not a word was spoken. Sadly, the report contains no mention of the outcome so we do not know if the woman was effectively treated or if the police were called.

What about taking the offensive against suspected witches? The most potent measure was to draw the witch's blood though many people were afraid to take such drastic action. And scratching or stabbing a witch was not easy and if the case came to court the severity of sentencing for assault was severe.

In one case in the magistrates court in the late 1800s a defendant said she would not have attacked the plaintiff had she not discovered that she was a witch. She had been suspicious of the woman for some time and had waited for an opportunity of resolving the matter. At last she succeeded in scratching the witch's arm with a crooked pin and when she saw there was no blood that was proof positive in her mind. She did not hold back and hit the suspected witch. The magistrates asked if the plaintiff had ever molested her and the defendant replied she had suspected her of doing many an unkindness to her and that she now knew that she had come in at the keyhole when her child was in his cradle and had caused him to have fits. At that time epilepsy was held to be a sure sign of bewitchment.

Ask any twenty-first century children what they know about witches and the answer will not vary much. They were vindictive old hags, they will tell you, cruel and frightening. They were ugly and deformed and through their magic powers they could harm any human being or animal they wished. They could fly through the air on broomsticks. And children are likely to accept the traditional explanation of how these wicked people became witches. All they needed to do was to go to church, to the communion service, and take the holy bread but not swallow it. After the service they would meet an old toad in the churchyard. And who was the toad? None other than the Devil in disguise meeting his new witch, perhaps to congratulate her on joining his ranks. These will be descriptions recognised by children who have never seen a witch, whose parents and grandparents will dismiss the whole witchcraft business as nonsense. The image, however, comes from a distant past, by word of mouth, through stories told in books and films.

From the records, most of those accused of witchcraft were above the age of fifty, a good age in times past. Small wonder then that they hobbled, were bent up, were frail. Perhaps they were not muttering spells to themselves. Perhaps they suffered from the onset of the various mental ailments which beset the old.

Many of these witches had long dispensed 'simples', herbal remedies to the sick. Some of them had for many years brewed up their own concoctions in their cottages. But what if their remedies failed? What if their patients died? What if a young woman in childbirth has been to see the person described as a 'wise woman'? Perhaps she has asked for advice, a potion to ease her discomfort. And what if this fails? What if she dies? Perhaps this is where the suspicion festers locally, so that children start calling names and their parents comparing notes. Such a progress from respected 'wise woman' to detested 'witch' is feasible.

Thomas Geering writing about Hailsham in the 1830s said that all of the so-called witches he had ever known had been poor. Those he had feared in his boyhood were all decrepit, housebound, shunned by children. One of them, so they had all believed, used her walking stick to ride to the moon on nightly errands of mischief. He says that responding to rumours she once said, 'If I was a witch, I would never want for snuff.' Such a humble want.

Whilst over the ages there are those who have involved themselves in the occult, some no doubt to some effect, it is difficult to accept that the majority of those accused of witchcraft were any more than the unfortunate victims of ignorance and superstition.

Cunning-folk and Counter-spells

From early times until the first thirty or forty years of the twentieth century there was often and especially in the remoter villages, a great dependency on the cunning-folk, people with a reputation for diagnosing and suggesting

magical charms for problems. Like the charmers, many were experienced herbalists, men and women who had over many years of visiting or being visited by the sick, picked up useful information and developed valuable treatments. They were trusted by those who had come to rely on them, an important element in effecting any kind of cure, as much today as in the past. Much to the dismay of the educated the spread of rational thought

seemed not to have filtered down to the labouring classes. The harshness of life, both rural and urban, right up to the twentieth century, cannot be too greatly emphasised. Their days dogged by misfortune, many of the poor maintained their faith in the magical beliefs their forefathers had always held and returned time and again to cunning-folk, to astrologers and fortune tellers, people who professed occult powers and who could provide comfort and succour that neither church nor state could offer.

Known variously as cunning-men and wise-women, conjurors, sorcerers and white witches, they had an acknowledged expertise in magic and through their beneficial magical practices they were believed able to repair bodily or mental disorders. They were fortune-tellers, locaters of lost and stolen property and animals, detectors of thieves, prescribers of love magic, advisers in business matters. Most important they were able to identify if spells had been placed on their clients and properties and if required could offer magical charms as counter measures. And even the police called on them when the solution of some or other offence seemed intractable.

Boys Firmin of Crowborough summed up the cunning-folk very fairly: 'Some were learned and profound, excellent mathematicians and exponents of physical laws; others were superficial, mere charlatans, who learned a few technical terms with which to astonish the ignorant, and whose knowledge extended no further than to repeat what others had said, or to copy what others did.' Perhaps that is true of many trades and professions.

A Hastings cunning-man named Zacharias is mentioned at a trial in 1593 at which. Elizabeth Drinkwater, a widow at Rye, gave evidence: 'She sayeth that she supposinge her childe to be bewytched by reason the same was very weake, she went to Hastinge to one Zacharias…whom she had heard to be a connynge man, to know of him what her child lacked, who told [her]. . . that one Mother Rogers had bewytched her child and gave her councell to fetch blood of her in takeinge a knyffe and to thrust it in her buttocke, but she tooke another corse for she prycked her in the hand and thereuppon presently her child took rest and 2 great gerles dyd heare when the said Zachary gave her that councell.'

Apparently Mrs Drinkwater could not bring herself to follow Mr Zacharias' advice to the last letter. The 'buttocke' was a step too far: she opted for the hand instead. In the subsequent court case, brought presumably by the injured woman, Mr Zacharias's books were confiscated and put in the custody of a clergyman.

Another early example of the work of a cunning-man at work, was again at Rye, where Henry Backbourne, described as 'chirurgion [surgeon] and occulist by his profession' was said that to be able to restore sight to the blind. One of his patients, Alice Stace, the 75 year old wife of a Hastings fisherman, had been blind in both eyes but could now see again. Three others, it was said, were 'yet alive, in good sort, can see, and goe about the towne without any guide.'

Charlotte Latham recorded the following about a nineteenth century cunning-woman approached by the mother of a boy with mouth ulcers which prevented him from eating or drinking. The cunning-woman said it was as bad a case of 'oral thrush' that she had ever seen. '"So",' says I to the child's mother, "Do you know of a left twin girl anywhere here about?"'

A 'left twin' was a surviving twin. For the treatment to work, however, this twin had to be of the opposite sex to the patient.

The cunning-woman continued: 'She said, "Yes, my cousin Eliza at the shop is a left twin." "Good," says I. "Take the boy down to her and ask her to blow into his mouth, and then to stop a minute; then to blow again, and stop a minute and then blow for the third time and the child will have no remains of the thrush tomorrow." ' Apparently the cure worked.

In cases of bewitchment cunning-folk were in great demand. Not only did they identify witches, their polar opposites, but they also cured the bewitched. When a Crowborough woman became seriously ill, her husband tried all kinds of remedies but had no success. He began to suspect Dame Killick, a reputed witch, who lived on Crowborough Common at Slaughterham Ghyll (Slapham Ghyll) of casting a spell on his wife. In some desperation he went to consult Mr Oakley at Tunbridge Wells. He explained his wife's worsening condition, saying that he feared she was bewitched. Oakley asked whether he would be able to recognise the witch if he saw a picture or image of her. When the man said that he would, Oakley produced some chemical ingredients in a cup and poured liquid on them. After this there was a fizzing and a hissing, and then yellow, blue and white fumes came from the cup. After it settled the liquid cleared. Oakley told the man to look into the cup. He did so, peering at the surface of the liquid, and finally he called out, 'I see her. It's Witch Killick. She is the person tormenting my wife.' He returned home with full instructions of how to exorcise the evil spirit from his wife.

Oakley's technique of scrying – what we might now call clairvoyance or clear vision – was common enough. Other cunning-folk used other kinds of reflective surface such as crystal balls, mirrors or smoked glass. Some would heat a horseshoe, plunge it into dirty water and then ask the client to identify the face appearing through the steam.

Of course, it is easy to suspect that people were gulled by Oakley and his kind. Were there really faces to be seen on surfaces, through steam and fumes? Was it all a matter of persuasion, of clever suggestion by the cunning-man? Was it all smoke and mirrors? Such trickery must have occurred in many cases. But could cunning-folk have got away with such trumpery all the time? Could Oakley and his like and all of their predecessors, thousands of them down the centuries, have carried out such deceits without being detected and denounced? Would they not have been quickly unmasked?

In fact it seems that these men and women were highly regarded in their communities. In 1750 Walter Gale, the Mayfield schoolmaster, referred to elsewhere in this book, recorded in his diary a visit from 'Mr Hassell the conjuror [who] brought a map with him he had made up of a farm belonging to Colonel Fuller.' Hassell had approached the schoolmaster to do some work on the map for him. They had lunch together. Perhaps this indicates that the Heathfield conjuror was recognised as a respectable sort of man.

Most of the cunning-folk were of somewhat higher social status than the charmers. For the most part they were male and usually skilled artisans, tradesmen, schoolmasters or farmers. Several of them accorded themselves the title 'Doctor.' Accounting themselves professionals, unlike the charmers, they charged for their services.

Often young men and women would want to know who they were to marry and how many children they might have. There was a cunning-woman at Bury who would tell young men or women whether their future spouses would be short or tall, rich or poor and dark or fair. But the procuring of love and marriage by magical means, described elsewhere in this book, was also possible. There were spells for love as for anything else.

A very important part of the cunning-folk's work involved astrology. They said they could 'rule the stars,' speaking of good and evil planets and carrying out their magic procedures according to the phases of the moon. They professed to be able to calculate charts of the heavens and certainly many of them possessed very impressive books on the subject.

The Crowborough cunning-man, Avory, was perhaps typical of the profession. He declared himself a reader of the planets, a teller of fortunes, a detector of thieves, one who could cast spells, a man who could explain to worried farmers why pigs did not fatten and who might be responsible for this.

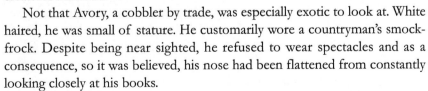

The story went that earlier in his life he had sold his soul to the Devil but when they had disagreed about the distribution of the profits, Avory had given up the connection. But Avory himself did not put this tale about: it seems to be just one of those embellishments to their life stories which such exotic creatures attracted.

Not that Avory, a cobbler by trade, was especially exotic to look at. White haired, he was small of stature. He customarily wore a countryman's smock-frock. Despite being near sighted, he refused to wear spectacles and as a consequence, so it was believed, his nose had been flattened from constantly looking closely at his books.

From these books Avory drew meaning from the positions of the planets, signs of the Zodiac, the divisions of the heavens and how these affected people's lives. Everything that concerned people could be learned from such study, he claimed. From birth dates and other information given him by those who came to consult him, Avory would make calculations, each of which required a diagram. Such esoteric matter, totally beyond the comprehension of the ordinary man, added to the magical aura, giving Avory the reputation of a man of distinct learning and wisdom. It must all have seemed so mysterious and mystical to the uninitiated and doubtless many who visited Avory were overcome with a sense of apprehension and bewilderment.

Yet Avory's knowledge appears to have been limited. People resorted to him with questions about sick pigs or lost money and girls always wanted to know about love and marriage and what the future held. The planets, Avory would say, held all the secrets and he was privy to them. His written charms, with their astrological symbols and their odd lines of Latin, were doubtless much prized. The mass of folk might be totally illiterate but even so a few words of dog-Latin had a cachet in their eyes.

But was Avory effective? That was the question. According to Boys Firmin he certainly was. 'Before you could tell him, he knew that you had lost those twelve chickens that you had been so carefully preserving for the higgler. He knew who had taken them, where they could be found, and whether you would get them back again.'

From time to time, Avory and others of his kind were asked to help the police in their investigations. Perhaps it would be cynical to suggest that on some occasions the police acquainted Avory with details of local crimes and suspects.

The most lucrative aspect of the work of cunning-folk was with those who believed themselves or their animals to be bewitched. Very often the most complex processes were involved. For example, in one early nineteenth century case, after selling his client a charm to wear against a spell cast by a witch, one cunning-man mixed herbs and spices in a half pint of gin. A tablespoonful of this mixture was to be taken at four specified times each day. In addition, each morning before taking any food, four tablets had to be swallowed. Then a powder mixed with a little honey was to be taken on twelve successive nights. Next, there followed a midnight ceremonial in which a few herbs, mixed with hay and a sprig of rosemary, were to be burnt during which time the two verses of the 68th psalm were to be read. 'Let God arise, and let his enemies be scattered: let them also that hate him flee before him. Like as the smoke of vanisheth, so shalt thou drive them away: and like as wax melteth at the fire, so let the ungodly perish at the presence of God.' This was followed by the Lord's Prayer.

Yet this ceremony did not ensure that the witch would not cast the same spell on the same victim again. To ensure that her power was ended for good and always the witch's blood had to be drawn just as Zacharias had proposed in Tudor times and countless others must have done centuries earlier. It was as a result of this advice that a nineteenth century woman, who had called in the cunning-man, ended up in a court of law along with her two daughters answering charges of assault.

Such attempts to draw a witch's blood as part of a cunning-man's counter-spell continued until the twentieth century. But increasingly the plaintiffs in court were not those who accounted themselves witches' victims but rather innocent people accused of witchcraft who had been stabbed with a knife or a nail or a pair of scissors.

Other methods might be necessary. Sometimes some local women might agree to meet for a cup of tea in the victim's home. The group might even  include the unsuspecting witch. Once the group had gathered and the tea was in the pot, everyone was asked to throw ends of their hair and some nail parings into the pot of boiling water. This counter-spell was expected to trap the witch for she would always shriek with pain in these circumstances. Sometimes a cunning-man was called in to supervise the ritual which was carried out in complete silence.

Of course the whole business was open to fraud and the Witchcraft Act of 1736 recognised this possibility. From then, although cunning-folk could no longer be charged with witchcraft they could be charged with fraud. There were countless cases of stringing along a gullible public with phoney astrological forecasts, false promises about prospective lovers, instances of more and more unnecessary and expensive consultations to resolve a particular problem.

The *Sussex Advertiser* seems to suggest that fraud had been perpetrated in Cuckfield in the summer of 1869 after a woman had been confined to her bed for several months and had had no satisfaction from any local doctor. She talked the matter over with her friends and they concluded that she must be possessed by an evil spirit. A local cunning-man was consulted and after considering the facts and studying the appropriate texts in his impressive books, he promised to exorcise the spirit. He explained that the charm he was to use was exceptionally potent and must therefore be carried out in the greatest secrecy. He had made calculations relating to planetary positions and had worked out that the most favourable time for his magic to be worked was on the following Saturday at midnight. He set about his preparations buying new pins for the witch-bottle which frequently featured in such cases.

At the arranged hour the friends of the afflicted woman came to her house in great secrecy. Certain ceremonial operations followed involving a pair of fire tongs and the pins which were placed in the bottle by the fire. For an hour the cunning-man addressed the spirit 'in a commanding tone', employing all sorts of unintelligible language. But the sick woman showed no signs of recovery. Some days after the ceremony the lady's friends, despite their promise to retain the utmost secrecy, decided to break their silence, though whether this led to any police intervention is not known. The cunning-man was later to claim that by breaking their promise not to speak about what they had witnessed, the charm which had required time to take effect had been broken. As a result, their friend was left in the same state as before.

Cunning-folk: villains, shysters, frauds, charlatans. They were called all of these names, many of them deservedly. But it is difficult to believe that most of them deceived those who sought their help. Had the majority of them been unreliable, would they have been able to gull so many down the centuries? Could our forefathers with their sometimes harsh and uneasy lives really afford to indulge themselves in ideas which were ineffective and fanciful? Have we lost genuine practitioners of magic in our sceptical age? And have we also lost the malevolent creatures who cast spells on our predecessors?

All superstitious nonsense? Are you sure?

Charms and Charmers

Seek out the doctor? Certainly not. At least, certainly not in the case of many people until the early twentieth century, especially those living in the country. Many relied on herbal folk medicines or harmless patent medicines along with laudanum. They would prefer to deal with the local charmer than send for a so-called doctor with all his new-fangled science. The charmers' old cures had been trusted for centuries. The following mid-nineteenth century case illustrates this rejection of the licensed medical man in favour of someone with the old knowledge.

A poor Sussex woman who had been very badly scalded refused to be attended to by the parish surgeon nor would she herself apply any remedy. She had absolute faith in the local charmer. As a consequence she remained in acute pain for several days until the following Sunday. Then the charmer came to the woman's bedside, 'bowed her head over the wound, crossed two of her fingers over it, and, after repeating some words to herself, huffed, or breathed quickly on it'. The woman's pain was instantly relieved.

The charmer could not have attended to the injured woman at any other time. Like many charmers she functioned effectively only at certain times and days. Some charmers insisted on working before sunrise, others at sunset: some were able to effect cures only on their own favoured day of the week, as did this woman.

This faith in the local charmer was still present in rural areas in the early decades of the twentieth century. The charmers lacked the hierarchy of skills and the range of magic solutions offered by the cunning-men and wise-women who dealt in more complex matters of magic. They did not claim to diagnose but they dealt with the consequences of accidents such as bleeding, burns, snake bites and natural diseases such as ringworm, toothache, scrofula and warts. There were times when they were called on to cure lameness, blindness, deafness, fits, palsy, dropsy and cancer. They did not, however, attempt to counter the effects of bewitchment.

There were both male and female charmers, the men usually rural craftsmen or small farmers. Strangely, with the exception of those who healed by touch, few were labourers. Within the rural areas they were easy of access and there was a certain protocol observed by both charmer and patient who was required never to use the terms 'please' or 'thank you' and never to consider offering cash in return for a cure. The charmer was considered to possess a divine gift which he was obliged to give freely, as a matter of course. That is not to say that the patients did not later express an unspoken gratitude, leaving perhaps some eggs or a basket of vegetables on the charmer's doorstep. But there had to be no acknowledgment that there was any relationship between the doorstep gift and the treatment.

In the 1880s Janet Steer, a shopkeeper in Malling Street, Lewes, had the gift of being able to cure warts. But it was a gift which cost her money, for rather than take payment she counted the warts and bought each one for a halfpenny before employing whatever method of curing she favoured.

Other charmers possessed secret written or oral charms which could be applied by the sufferers themselves. The different treatments for warts illustrate how the charmers went about their work. There were those who simply passed their hands over the affected area. Others rubbed the warts in some decaying organic matter – a snail perhaps or a pea pod. Some charmers favoured using a stone or a stick. Others used several stones, rubbing each wart with a different stone. After this treatment, charmers would sometimes put the stones in a bag and leave it on the highway. Whoever picked up the bag would inherit the warts. There were others who pricked the warts with pins which were then stuck into the trunk of an ash tree. As they became embedded in the bark the warts were expected to disappear. Or a small piece of meat, stolen by the charmer from the sufferer's own larder, was buried in secret by the roadside. The expectation was that as it decayed so would the warts.

One woman whom Charlotte Latham visited in the Fittleworth neighbourhood said that she had been taught about magic charms by a man from Midhurst who swore her to secrecy. Such charms with their associated rituals were usually handed on orally at the death bed to friends or family members, not unlike the manner in which those called witches handed over their secret powers to their successors.

While living, charmers were reluctant to divulge the secret which had been passed on to them. Only in the last moments of their lives did they consider it safe to hand on the mystery. To do so earlier could weaken not only the power of the charm but that of the charmer, who would then be at the mercy of the recipient.

Nevertheless, on condition that she never told it to anyone else, Mrs Latham was let in on the secret. There was a neat distinction in her informant's mind. In this charmer's view, writing was not the same as telling and so, only 'after she had assured me more than once that there was no harm in using it, for it was only a blessing and had nothing to do with witchcraft,' the charmer gave her enquirer her charm for burns in written form. It ran:

> *There came two angels from the north,*
> *One was fire and one was frost.*
> *Out fire, in frost –*
> *In the name of the Father, Son and Holy Ghost.*

During the blessing the charmer had to place crossed fingers over the injured part. Remarkably, this particular word-charm, which had to be repeated three times, operated almost word for word in other parts of the British Isles save that the angels in some cases come out of the west or the east.

The same informant mentioned another thrice-repeated incantation used for a variety of injuries.

> *Our Saviour Christ was of a pure Virgin born*
> *And he was crowned with a thorn;*
> *I hope it may not rage nor swell;*
> *I trust in God it may do well.*

This same woman had inherited from her mother a charm for viper bites and although she had lost this she recalled having once tried it successfully on a young man who had been bitten. His arm had swollen terribly and the doctor could do him no good. She had pronounced her blessing over his injury and, so she claimed, he had soon recovered.

Unsurprisingly, the clergy were not especially enthusiastic about charmers and their activities. Despite the fact that many charms sounded essentially Christian in form, comprising short prayers or stories of Christ and the disciples, some regarded charming as no more than witchcraft, some evil inspired by the Devil. But as the charms contained references to the Holy Trinity, and as the Bible itself carried examples of the effectiveness of such cures, that was quite enough for many charmers, who defended their use of charms by saying that they were only 'blessings'. After all, did they not mention Christ and the saints and angels?

Not that Mrs Latham was entirely satisfied with these 'blessings'. Perhaps that is not surprising considering her husband's vocation. On one occasion she complains 'that thousands in our civilised England are practising observances more grossly superstitious [than the Kaffirs and Negroes in Africa] and believing just as firmly in their efficacy'.

Years earlier, in 1802, A.F.M. Willich's *Domestic Encyclopaedia* had condemned 'any dependence upon charms and such occult modes of curing disease. They have been adopted by the ignorant multitude and they have more frequently failed than succeeded.'

Disapproved of or not, the ministrations of charmers, men and women who regarded themselves as no more than mediums through which their powers were channelled, were still being sought out in the 1930s. During this period there was a serious outbreak of diphtheria, and anxious parents in Sussex, desperate to protect their children, visited charmers. One of these – not strictly a charmer, for this woman charged for her services – tied a hazel twig around the children's necks and whenever this procedure failed they were made to swallow a spoonful of stewed mouse. When the local doctor heard what was happening to his patients he called in the police to put a stop to the charmer's activities.

One charmer, a woman, had the ability to cure giddiness in cattle. On one occasion a farmer had come from a distance to beg her to save the life of a valuable cow that had been taken suddenly ill. She had said her blessing and before the farmer reached home the animal had recovered from whatever had ailed it. While there is no relatively recent example of distance-curing in Sussex, there were cases of human ringworm in the West Country being cured by telephone in the 1950s. Once, when the charmer was ill in bed and unable to visit the farm, it is said that a sick cow was taken to the telephone to hear the charm.

It is not intended to describe the treatment prescribed for every ailment suffered by humans and animals in earlier times. There is to be no listing of folk medicines, for that area has already been thoroughly covered by other writers. This chapter, then, is to be limited to those cures which appear to have no scientific backing and to have been carried out by those with no formal medical training and whose skills were relatively narrow.

One ailment particularly rife in times past was whooping cough. This wretched illness, with a cough that might last up to three months, was highly infectious and often fatal to babies. There used to be regular epidemics and it is not surprising that in addition to the many herbal remedies available this ailment resulted in charmers prescribing a huge variety of cures.

In the late seventeenth century Richard Stapley, who lived at Hickstead Place, wrote one of these cures in his diary: 'Take three field mice, flay them, draw them and roast them and let the party afflicted eat it; dry the others in the oven until they crumble to a powder, and put a little of the powder in what the patient drinks at night and in the morning.'

Others would have the mouse boiled in milk and another recommendation recorded by William Parish, the vicar of Selmeston, was to roast the mouse alive. He was wryly dubious about the effect of this particular approach.

'Whether it is really good for the whooping cough or not, I cannot say,' the vicar comments, 'but I am sure it must be bad for the mouse.'

As a cure, live spiders wrapped inside a pill of cobwebs had its supporters as did a silk bag filled with hair from the cross on a donkey's neck. In this cure the patient sat on the donkey facing backwards and was sent to a certain spot three times on three successive days. On the other hand there were those who favoured eating bread and butter from a family whose heads were named John and Joan.

Or what about asking a man on a piebald horse what was his recommended choice of cure? A man living in Petworth who owned such a horse was constantly asked for his recommendations by anxious mothers. One day he would plump for ale and butter, another day for honey and vinegar. It seems that he said the first thing that entered his head but apparently his success rate was high. Confidence is all in matters medical.

Before the twentieth century goitre was a not uncommon complaint. In 1831 a woman climbed the scaffold at Horsham where John Holloway, Brighton's first trunk murderer, was hanged. She was allowed to stroke his throat, acknowledged as a way in which to cure her condition.

One omnipresent children's complaint which Charlotte Latham refers to was bedwetting, and she deals with it with all the delicacy that one might expect from the wife of a Victorian clergyman.

'When a poor child has in vain been whipped and scolded for the nightly repetition of a certain involuntary offence,' she says, 'in the last resort one of the following remedies may be tried. On the day appointed for the funeral of a person not of the same sex as the child, while the first part of the burial service is being read within the church, the child is to be taken to the open grave, and is there to do that which constituted the original offence. My informant told me that, although she had taken her own little boy to the churchyard, he had not the courage to carry out the first remedy, so she tried the second, with complete success. It consists in the child's first going alone to fix upon an ash tree suitable for the purposes of the charm, and going afterwards upon another day, without divulging his intention, to gather a handful of the ash seeds, which he must lay with the left hand in the hollow of the right arm. Thus are they to be carried home, and then they are to be burned to ashes. The charm is then completed by the child performing the same ceremony over the embers on the hearth, which in the former remedy it was to go through at the open grave.'

A necklace of moles' feet for toothache was much favoured and this remedy was said to be equally helpful for rheumatism. Some wore round their necks the feet of rabbits and hares, though some, more fastidious perhaps, preferred to carry a double hazelnut in the pocket.

Mrs Latham found a *Book of Common Prayer* which had previously belonged to a Sussex labourer who had written on the flyleaf: 'As Peter sat weeping on a marble stone, Christ came by and said unto him, 'Peter, what hailest [ails] thou.' Peter answered and said unto him, 'My Lord and my God, my tooth eaketh [aches].' Jesus said unto him, 'Arise, Peter, and be thou hole; and not thee only but all them that carry these lines for my sake, shall never have the tooth ake. Joseph Hyman's his book.'

A written charm was often worn on a piece of string or ribbon round the neck and its presence was expected to cause warts to disappear. But in any case warts come and go and it might have been time rather than the charm which had the desired result.

The following extract comes from the magazine *Sussex Life* in 1973: 'One of the best known remedies for many ills, and one still very much in use, is fasting spittle. This was used for scurvy, skin blemishes, warts, bites, and sore eyes. A girl in my class (c.1910 - 1915) who had weak eyes, under the doctor's orders, wetted her eyes each morning with fasting spittle . . . I have used fasting spittle for warts and last year a man told me that he had cured himself of what a surgeon had described as a skin cancer by wetting it each morning with fasting spittle.'

This apparently contains more saline matter than ordinary saliva, though whether this scientific element was known to the charmers is unlikely. But what an excellent all-purpose remedy at the tip of the tongue! And it was known in AD 70 – and presumably long before – when it was referred to in *Mark 7:32-35*: 'And they bring unto him one that was deaf, and had an impediment in his speech . . . And he took him aside from the multitude, and put his fingers into his ears, and he spit, and touched his tongue: and saith unto him, "Ephphatha", that is, "Be opened".'

Only a few years later Pliny, the Roman scholar, was to urge the use of fasting spittle for ophthalmia which could be cured by anointing the eyes each morning. And so these cures meander their way across the world, ending up in various lands and whilst they undergo some changes they are essentially the same.

Some charmers, especially the seventh sons or daughters, were believed to possess an innate healing touch. They would stroke the affected area with fasting spittle and prayer. This group of charmers tended not to use verbal formulae either written or spoken.

Scrofula, characterised by running sores on the neck, was also known as King's Evil because the monarchs of Britain and France claimed to be able to heal it by touch. Alternatively those affected might wish to visit Ashburton Church where at one time the blood-stained shirt worn by Charles I at his execution and the sheet that later covered his body were kept. It was thought that having absorbed royal blood merely to touch them would cure scrofula. Yet was it such a strange thought? It would certainly have been recognised as not unusual within the Roman Catholic church, where the blood and bones of saints were so prized.

In Sussex, the intermittent feverish chills of ague were very common. 'Old Johnny,' the old folk would say, 'has been running his finger down my back,' describing the effect of the ailment also known as Axey, Johnny, Old Johnny and Lord John.

On the 29 April 1858, the diary entry of the Revd John Coker Egerton,

Rector of Burwash, reads: 'We have a great number of ague cases this winter and spring; more I am told than have ever been known simultaneously before.'

Ague was a regular snatcher of lives. According to Willich's *Domestic Encylopaedia*, it 'more frequently attacked men than women, the young than the old, the poor than the rich.' He goes on to say, 'The employments of the male sex, especially at the time of youth, subject them to causes which more particularly predispose them to that disease, such as cold moist air, wet feet, long exposure to rain, and wet clothes; whereas females and the aged of both sexes, keep more within doors.'

He suggests a number of remedies: powdered snakeskin in a glass of brandy and water; two spoonsful of sage juice mixed with vinegar; laxatives and then he points out with some apparent enthusiasm that many patients had been cured by common spiders, three or four of them with the legs cut off and mixed with honey. The latter remedy is more or less the same as that which John Wesley suggested fifty years earlier: 'For the ague swallow six middling sized pills of cobweb at stated times.'

Years later, towards the end of the century, Mr Warter, the vicar of West Ferring, 'testified to the prevalence among the peasantry thereabouts of such superstitions as the following. Pills made of spiders' webs are prescribed by unqualified practitioners as a remedy for ague.' Not that it was obligatory to be swallowed as a pill. The squeamish could place the spider in a nutshell and wear it round the neck in a bag of black silk.

There were so many other suggested remedies for ague: for example, eating seven sage leaves after fasting on each of seven mornings. One girl was advised to put a caterpillar in a box and carry it in her pocket. When the caterpillar wasted away, she was told, her fevers would pass off.

Despite the unlikelihood of a cure from such recipes, there was still a strong mistrust of 'doctors' stuff'. One mother refused medicine for her child, suffering from ague. No medicine was any use, she claimed. She had no faith in anything unless it had passed three times under the belly of an ass. She said: 'It is something about Our Saviour's riding on an ass into Jerusalem. And about the cross that wasn't on the ass's back before and has been there ever since that time.'

Unlike other cures, there appear to have been no spoken charms for ague. These were always written down and passed on from one sufferer to another, not unlike a chain letter. Sometimes the text was secret, placed in an envelope to be worn round the neck but never read by the wearer. William Parish writes of one triangular piece of paper with the words visible, it too worn round the neck. This charm read:

> *Ague, ague, I thee defy.*
> *Three days shiver,*
> *Three days shake,*
> *Make me well for Jesus' sake.*

The *West Sussex Gazette* in 1964 carried an interesting item. An interviewee told a reporter: 'My granny said as she'd seed a old man tied to that tree by a rope as he'd got the other end round his waist and he ran round and round the tree till the rope was tight, and then he went the other way till 'twas loose again, an' called out three times: "Ague, ague I do thee defy, Make me well for Jesu's sake." An' granny said he was better after.'

Yet others favoured wood from the gallows or a gibbet as a cure for ague. In 1734 a pedlar, Jacob Harris, faced a charge of triple murder in the course of a burglary at an inn on Ditchling Common. The jury found him guilty, 'not having the fear of God before him but being moved or seduced by the Devil on the 26th May with a knife value twopence did cut the throat of Richard Miles making two mortal wounds each of the length of five inches and at the depth of two inches of which he died on the 30th May.' But on the same occasion he had also slain Miles's wife and maidservant. After he was hanged at Horsham, his body was gibbetted on Ditchling Common but the gibbet, Jacob's Post as it came to be called, was thought to possess 'a power of enchantment'. Not only was the hanged man's body and later his skeleton touched by women seeking to cure their barrenness, but others cut off pieces of the gibbet to carry in their pockets.

These splinters of wood were regarded as a sovereign cure for ague as well as neuralgia and toothache. One old lady living on Ditchling Common for more than 80 years carried a piece of the gibbet long after all her teeth were gone.

In 1881 Jacob's Post was still held to have curative powers. In that year a doctor, called to attend a patient suffering from epilepsy, was told by an old Newick native: 'Ah, sir, pity, surely he hadn' a bit of Jacob's Post in his pocket.

They do say no-one wouldn't never have this here falling sickness if he had a bit of Jacob's Post, like, about him. Why, sir, people comes miles and miles from Ashdown Forest way to get a bit of that post so as they shouldn't fall in these here fits.'

Wearing a holed stone round the neck as protection against the ague seems rather dull after the other more exciting kinds of cure.

Epilepsy was often attributed to witchcraft, possibly in part because sufferers gnashed their teeth, which witches were also supposed to do. Some charmers suggested as a cure a ring made of six silver sixpenny coins donated by six bachelors.

For rheumatism which was especially common among the poor there were several remedies, some patently absurd. A clergyman found an old woman seated on the edge of her chair and told her that she was in danger of slipping off. She said she was quite safe and that she was sitting in that way to make room for the bellows behind her in the chair. She said leaning against the bellows was a fine thing for rheumatism. It wasn't there as a support but rather as a charm to rid her of the ailment.

And the following remedy for rheumatism was reported in various parts of the country in the late nineteenth century. 'My grandmother,' one woman said, 'used often to tell me that in her young days there was an old Brighton woman who said, "Please as how I gets confarmed as often as ever I can, 'cos as how I hears 'tis good for the rheumatiz".' By which she meant, presumably, that she attended communion whenever she felt a twinge.

A woman speaking to William Parish, her local vicar, had another remedy though her particular ailment is rather confused.

'There's so many new complaints nowadays to what they used to be,' she told him. 'There is this here rheumatism there's so much talk about. When I was a gal 'twas the rheumattics and I doan't know as there's much odds in it now – naun but you wants to cure the rheumatism you wants a lot of doctor's stuff; but for my part, if ever I be troubled with the rheumattics (and I be quite eat up otherwhile) I goos out and steals a tater, and carries it in my pocket till the rheumattics be gone.'

An elder stick with three, five or seven knots in the pocket seems to have been a trusted rheumatics cure for some, while others swore by placing the shoes at bedtime in the form of a cross.

More enlightened folk were often horrified at the sheer ignorance and superstition they encountered. One remedy, still commonly used for the rupture in children in the late nineteenth century, roused their scorn. A child suffering from a hernia had to be passed nine times at sunrise on nine successive days through a cleft in a bough of a sapling ash or oak. The sapling had to be of strong growth and the cleft cut with an axe. The child was carried to the tree, attended by nine people, each of whom had to pass it through the cleft from west to east. On the ninth morning the solemn ceremony was concluded by binding the tree tightly with the cord. It was expected that as the cleft closed so the child's rupture would heal.

In the Petworth area there were several bound boughs through which parents had recently passed their children. The owners of the trees always had to grant permission for the rite to be carried out and had to promise the child's parents that the tree would never be cut down during the child's lifetime. If this promise were broken, it was said, the infirmity would return.

Some remedies were easy to apply. For instance a lady in Mayfield told how she had had her stye treated by a nurse who rubbed it with a borrowed wedding ring. No other kind of ring would serve the purpose, the nurse told her. Of course gold wedding rings were not difficult to get hold of, but a cure for gangrene seems more complex. For that, a nest of bluebottles placed on the affected part of the body was required. As for hydrophobia – and newspapers of a hundred and fifty years ago carry regular stories of mad dogs on the loose – it was suggested that 'a slice of the liver of the dog that bit you, boiled and eaten' would have the desired effect. Those suffering from boils were carried through an arch of brambles and those with consumption swallowed toads and frogs. And even in 1978 a correspondent to the *Sussex Express* comments, 'I am told that Sussex folk believe that verdigris from church bells will cure the shingles.'

Is it so remarkable that such curious beliefs existed? It was only in the mid-Victorian period that medical men managed to shake off their somewhat louche reputations, their low-life associations with barbers and resurrection men. Even if at last they were becoming socially acceptable, on almost equal terms with parsons and lawyers, their training was a hit-and-miss affair. The apprentice-medico picked up his knowledge and earned his reputation by a process of observation, practice, discussion, guesswork, study, trial and error, and good and bad luck. Perhaps it made them no better than the village charmers and, in fact, in some cases, decidedly worse.

Working conditions were often responsible for many of the ailments. Diarrhoea was attributable to long hours of labour in sodden fields. Bad housing, as might be expected, generated all manner of diseases, according to the Poor Law Commissioners: '. . . fevers of every type, catarrh, rheumatism, scrofula and phthisis, which from their frequent intermarriages and their low diet, abound so largely among the poor.'

Many field workers suffered from chronic rheumatism, a consequence of their constant walking from an early age in heavy hobnailed boots across rough, uneven ground. Often their only protection from the elements was a sack worn over their head and shoulders.

By the end of the nineteenth century and beyond, school logbooks in Sussex frequently refer to the children's absences and reveal a litany of complaints: bronchitis, scarlet fever, measles, ague, typhoid fever, chicken pox, ringworm, mumps, whooping cough, chilblains, carbuncles, boils, smallpox and something referred to as 'breaking out' on the face. These are chronicles and epidemics which ate into the lives of whole families for weeks and months,

Dead Man's Hand. In former times women would press the hand of a newly-executed felon to their throats as a cure for goitre.

46

and what could any doctor suggest to these poor folk? Better food? Another cottage? Improved working conditions?

Although the stethoscope was invented in 1819, it was not in universal use for many years. The heart was sometimes checked by the doctor putting his ear to the chest and it was for reasons of delicacy when dealing with ladies with such conditions that he carried with him a silk handkerchief, so that embarrassment could be kept to a minimum. Until the 1860s there was no clinical thermometer in general use, nor had the hypodermic syringe been invented. Laudanum was used to anaesthetise patients. Small wonder in a world of hacksaws, that the patients died of shock. At least the charmer's treatments rarely resulted in death.

Can it be wondered at, this reliance on the charmers? Only as the nineteenth century progressed were calls for their services reduced, presumably as people gradually gained confidence in trained doctors.

Some people abandoned the charmer but never went to a doctor. They relied upon their own remedies, often handed down over generations. In 1964 the *West Sussex Gazette* picked up such a remedy from one of its readers: 'When there's flu about, I puts a plate of cut-up onion in every room. That's what keeps colds away. All the cold germs goos into them.'

Well, perhaps that was as useful as other wonder remedies suggested through the media today.

Protecting the Home

Belief in witchcraft did not end with the passing of the Witchcraft Act in 1736 – at least, not as far as the less well educated were concerned. The following paragraph written by a rather disdainful Sussex correspondent in 1919 confirms the continued hold of witchcraft on the popular imagination:

'There is a woman, still living, 73 years of age, who has a profound belief in witchcraft. She constantly boils pins in urine, and stops up all the windows and cracks in her cottage to draw the man to her door that was doing her harm. This man, she declares, "seeds" her garden to prevent her fowls from laying eggs. She met the man once, but he only made faces at her, she declares, so she had to boil some more pins.'

What is evident is that the woman, believing that she had had a spell placed on her, was preparing a witch bottle. This was considered the most active counter to a witch's spell. It would work even if the identity of the witch was not known. The bottle, either of stoneware or glass, was intended to represent the witch's bladder. It was filled with the bewitched person's urine, hair and nail clippings, along with sharp objects such as thorns and pins. It was then buried under the hearth or at the house entrance and even in stables and cow-houses as a permanent obstruction to evil spirits.

Charlotte Latham was once told by one of her informants that she had seen a quart bottle filled with pins on a cottage hearth at West Dean. She was told not to touch the bottle because it was red hot and if she did so she would spoil the spell. The woman said that her daughter was afflicted with falling fits (epilepsy) and the doctor had done her no good. She went to a wise-woman who after payment told her that people afflicted with falling fits were deemed bewitched. She was told to get as many pins as would fill a quart bottle and then to stand it close to the fire. All doors were locked and windows barred and every other hole blocked up to make sure that the witch could not enter. The heat of the fire was regulated according to whether slow or rapid torture of the witch was required. Trapped outside in agony, and desperately trying to stop the torture being inflicted on her, the witch was forced to remove the spell. At least that is how the story was related.

A local cunning-man or wise-woman sometimes carried out this kind of ritual either in complete silence or with the recitation of a charm, but victims often performed the operation alone or in the company of a few neighbours and friends.

When the hearth of a house in Pulborough was taken up during repairs, one of the builders found a bottle in which were 200 pins, each one being bent or twisted. The hearth was considered an ideal location for a bottle as witches or their familiars could slip into a house by the chimney. Thought to be equally vulnerable, the doors were guarded too, bottles being placed under the floorboards or flagstones at the entry to houses.

An observer in 1846, visiting a cottage in Herstmonceux, saw a bag, carefully tied up and hanging from the clock. He was told that it contained Good Friday's bread, one bun from the batch baked on that day, which, when grated and taken in water, was good for the whooping cough, the fevers and other ailments that children were subject to, and this remedy was effective for a whole twelve months. Was this one of the earliest examples of mould quite unconsciously used as an antibiotic?

It was not unusual to find these buns on mantelpieces, some people claiming that it protected the house from fire and storm while others asserted that, left outside by the front door, the bread protected the house from all evil.

But supposing a spell had been cast. Or rather, supposing someone suspected that a spell had been cast upon him. What then? Possibly some new charm would be added. Perhaps the heart of a sheep might be stuck with pins – a hint here of the power of metal against evil – and hung over the chimney. The expectation was that as the heart withered so would the power of the spell, and eventually the sufferer would recover.

On floors, whether earth, oak-boarded or stone-flagged, were often strewn sprigs of verbena and twigs of elder and rowan, all possessing protective qualities. And there, around where the baby's cot might stand, yarrow, regarded as especially potent against witches, was scattered.

Mrs Latham, writing in Fittleworth in the 1870s, and as sceptical as ever, described 'an old woman in Tillington parish [who] keeps, with religious care, a printed copy of the apocryphal letter of our Lord to Abgarus, King of Edessa, which she bought from a travelling man (that is, a pedlar) who told her if she stuck it up on her kitchen wall, it would preserve her and her home from witchcraft and the evil eye.'

It was easy enough to sneer at this so-called witchcraft, but look at what happened when the lady of a house in East Harting reprimanded her servant girl and sent off with a flea in her ear an old woman who had been telling the girl's fortune. Such stuff and nonsense, the girl's employer must have said. And don't encourage such people, bringing them to the door like that. But almost immediately, according to local tradition, a shower of hot flints rained down on the house smashing all of the windows.

Elsewhere inside a house there might be an old shoe, either nailed to or hidden inside the wall or up the chimney, in the attic or under the floorboards. In 1934, under the stairs of a very old Sussex house, a pair of ladies' well preserved brown cowhide shoes from the time of Charles II was found. Why the shoe was deemed a protective token is unclear. Nevertheless, shoes hidden in this way have been found in houses all over the country. The Stag Inn at Hastings has on display a couple of mummified cats found inside the walls during the First World War. Presumably they were placed there as some kind of charm against mice and rats.

As a further precaution some of the cooking utensils might bear specific marks, sometimes of a religious nature, for witches were not above leaving poisons or drugs to take advantage of unsuspecting householders.

In some homes, a sickle or some other iron implement was hung over the bedhead, for witches and evil spirits could not withstand the power of iron. Some people hung up glass balls, sometimes used by fishermen as fishing floats, but which were also regarded as powerful deflectors of evil. In addition these formed part of cunning-folk's clairvoyance apparatus. Today you'll find the descendants of these glass balls hanging from Christmas trees.

Horseshoes, that most instantly recognisable symbol of good luck, were commonly hung on walls and doors. Today, we see them nailed on back doors and representations of them on wedding cakes and birthday cards and on scores of similar printed productions. The real thing was much more highly prized if it was discovered by chance, in consequence of which it was said to be ten times more potent. While the horse itself was always a powerful symbol, the horseshoe was held to be extremely lucky because of the material of which it was made. It was the metal rather than the U-shaped object which was of value.

This notion of the horseshoe containing good fortune only if it was placed upright, is a popular misconception. In former times the horseshoe was not intended simply to promote generalised good luck or meant in some kind of congratulatory way for a promotion at work or a removal to a new house. Its intention was to protect the household and to repulse the Devil, witches and evil spirits, for none of them was thought able to withstand the power of iron.

Even if a householder had planted witch bottles at each of the vulnerable entries to his home, by doors and chimneys in particular, and even if he ensured that there were protective tokens such as plants, grasses and Good Friday bread strewn around the house, these did not totally safeguard his property. People were often so careless. Burn the boiling milk and the cow could dry up. And as for the hens, here is one woman's complaint:

'Well,' she said, 'two years ago I had four hens laying at Christmas time when hens are worth having. And two gentlemen who were snipe shooting came in for breakfast. I boiled four eggs for them, two apiece. When they'd finished, what do you think they did? Threw the shells in the fire. The next morning there wasn't a single egg laid nor one the next day nor the next week. Never throw an eggshell on the fire.'

It was not enough to protect the inside of the home. The outside was equally important. In the garden, for instance, among the medicinal herbs and vegetables, the wary cottager might plant periwinkle, wild garlic and verbena, all of these disliked by witches. He might grow marigolds and indeed any yellow flowers, for this colour also served as a deterrent. Blue scabious, a plant with healing properties, was also much favoured. John Gerard in his *Herball* written in 1597 says 'the greater part of the root seemeth to be bitten away; old fantastick charmers report that the Devil did bite it for envie, because it is an herb that hath so many good virtues and it is so beneficial to mankind.'

When, in the morning, horses were found in the stable with their manes tangled, their flanks sweaty and dirty, their owners often concluded that they had been hag-ridden – that is, ridden in the night by witches or perhaps fairies. Perhaps more likely the horses had been out with smugglers. The floors of barns were often covered with bracken or heather, but there was holly, too, all of these intended to prevent horses being hag-ridden. Another method used to protect the animals from hag-riding was to hang holed stones, known also as hag-stones, in the stable. Robert Herrick's lines written in the mid-seventeenth century, offer a further alternative remedy:

Hang up hooks, and shears to scare
Hence the hag, that rides the mare,
Till they be all over wet,
With the mire and the sweat:
This observed, the manes shall be
Of your horses, all knot-free.

Horse brasses, highly polished, though not just for decoration, were considered very effective against evil intruders, as were horse skulls nailed to the wall. And when the animals went out to work they were often adorned not solely with brasses but with chaplets of foxglove, ivy, rowan and, though dangerous, deadly nightshade, round their necks to protect them against witches' tricks. Sometimes, to reinforce the protection, a sprig of the reputedly luck-bringing ash was tied to the horns of cattle. Incidentally, ash also offered the same security to humans, and many people carried a piece of ash twig in their pockets.

One of the most difficult times for country folk was when their animals fell sick, for they had only the most rudimentary knowledge of appropriate treatment. When the pig failed to fatten, when the cow dried up and the horse had colic or cough, their owners were at a loss and extremely anxious. The horse could be the most important economic asset that a man possessed. But not far behind, especially for the poor, were the two major meat and dairy producers, the pig and the cow. The pig, nourished for six or so months on small potatoes and family scraps, was usually bought in the spring and killed in the winter. That animal would feed a family for nearly a year, its rancid lard and its ever hardening, ever discolouring flesh, served up at some time each day. The milk from the cow made the butter and cheese which might be sold or bartered.

So the threat of the death of one of these precious animals was a source of alarm. Witches had a tendency to harm animals and the pigs were considered a prime target. They were noted for their erratic behaviour when ill, and it was this which sometimes convinced their owners that their pigs had been 'overlooked'. One protective measure was to pierce the animal's ear and insert a small twig of hellebore.

Then there were the charms. The Sussex Archaeological Society's collections contain documents written in the late eighteenth century by Timothy Butt, a Tillington farmer. His
spelling and syntax may be awry and even the particulars of his charms a shade obscure, but the Christian faith is evident in what he writes:

'For a bullock that is stung by an adder take salt and fresh grees [grease] and anoint the beast from the heart and say these words: Simon Joan Hunt why wouldst thou thy servant thou strongest thou my man. I wish it was thy man take Salt and Smare [smear] and lay it to thy Speer. In the name of the Father and the Son and the Holy Ghost, Amen.'

Mr Butt goes on: 'For a bullock that is sprung say the Words, Our Blessed Saviour for his Sons sake Pray Down the Blader [bladder], Blow that he may break. In the Name of the Father and of the Son and of the Blessed Trinetey. Saved may this Black Bullock be – or let the colour be what will Name it. Then say the Lord's Prayer and so say it three times.'

Some charmers held that their charms worked only when they knew the name of the man or the animal they were called upon to cure. In the above case it seems that it was enough to pronounce the colour of the animal.

Presumably Timothy Butt's charms were handed down in oral form and were over time converted into gobbledegook. Nevertheless he had faith in them, and doubtless other farmers had a strong belief in equally distorted charms.

Out in the fields, the animals had to continue being protected. In the eighteenth century a huge elm tree near Ditchling Beacon was laden with dead animals hanging by the leg from the branches. This kind of propitiation from local farmers might have been an ancient echo of long-gone sacrifices to the Anglo-Saxon god, Odin. On the other hand, as a farmer's wife has recently suggested, it might have been just a plain common-sense way of getting an infected beast off pasture land.

And just for luck, just to throw the Devil or his minions off the scent, ploughmen were known to plough crooked furrows when the new season began. Others threw into the first furrow of the day a small piece of bread or cheese or plum pudding or whatever 'levenses their wives had sent them off with. One of these men, in the 1920s, when asked by an interested onlooker why he had thrown down a scrap of food in this way was unable to say more than that it was for good luck. He'd always done it. Everybody did, he said.

Certainly it all seems to have been a life under threat for so many people whose superstitious beliefs must have caused them so much anxiety. Even as late as 1957 a lady from Battle was moved to write to *Woman's Own* magazine: 'I was taking down the cobwebs in a stable preparatory to whitewashing it when one of the milk roundsmen told me that if cobwebs were taken down in a stable a horse would go lame. Sure enough, a few days later, one of the horses was lame.'

So there, she seems to be saying, there must be something in these old stories. Could happenings like this always be a matter of coincidence?

Seeking Love, Finding Marriage

It's a young woman's constant question: Who am I going to marry? What is he going to be like? But in the past there was a belief that a girl could, by observing specific rituals, actually find out in advance the identity of her intended.

Charlotte Latham was well aware of how some local girls tried to resolve the question.

'Should a girl wish to ascertain what will be the personal appearance of her future husband,' she wrote, 'she must sit across a gate or stile and look steadfastly at the first new moon that rises after New Year's Day.

'She must go alone and must not have confided her intention of doing so to anyone and when the moon appears it is thus apostrophised:

All hail to thee, moon! All hail to thee!
I pray thee, good moon, reveal to me
This night who my husband must be.

'I know of no recent instance of this charm being tried,' says Mrs Latham, 'but I hear that the new January moon is still watched by our Sussex maidens, who, shivering with cold and fear, see the likeness of the future husband come.'

Now this is an entry into the occult. This is quite alarming stuff. Little wonder the girls shivered with fear. They were entering an unknown realm, one quite disturbing, using spells which many girls abandoned half way through for fear of what they thought was happening or what they thought might happen. For how could a distant lover be brought into the here and now, up to a moonlit gateway? It wasn't normal: it wasn't natural. What might occur? No wonder so many girls did not wait to find out.

If this particular mode of working out who was to be the future husband failed, there were other even more alarming rituals which girls engaged in. Several of these involved incantations and two of them required visits to a graveyard.

In the first of these graveyard visits, the girl was to pluck the leaves of a yarrow plant growing on a young man's grave and then repeat the following words, bolstered by an appeal to a higher authority:

'Yarrow, sweet Yarrow, the first that I have found,
In the name of Jesus Christ, I plucked it from the ground;
As Joseph loved sweet Mary, and took her for his dear,
So in a dream this night, I hope, my true love will appear.'

But supposing her husband-to-be did not appear in a dream? What if there was no sign of yarrow anywhere in the graveyard? Or even if there were, what if it grew only on the grave of an old person? No need to give up hope. She could return to the graveyard, this time with a handful of hemp seed. Yes, hemp, grown for centuries under the express command of Queen Elizabeth I to provide rope for the navy and for the hangman and available in pretty well every village.

Once in the graveyard, the girl had to sprinkle the seed, all the while reciting:

'Hemp seed, I sow thee,
Hemp seed, I sow thee;
And he that is my true love
Come after me and mow thee.'

Once she had sown the seed she was to look over her left shoulder and she could expect to see the figure of a man mowing as he followed her. That would be the wraith, the ghostly projection, of her future husband. This spell was said to work only on certain days deemed appropriate for divining the future –

Midsummer's Eve and St John's Eve, the 23rd and 24th June.

Wasn't this ritual even more unsettling than sitting on a gate or stile? Here, in a graveyard, wasn't the girl in a more frightening situation with the shadowy figure behind her appearing to cut down the newly planted, newly grown hemp? It would take an extremely courageous young woman to sit this out.

Another strategy: just before midnight, and again on St John's Eve, girls used to wash their blouses and hang them out to dry in front of the kitchen fire. Then, leaving the kitchen door wide open, they would sit in silence, waiting for the wraith to come in and turn the blouse. One woman told Mrs Latham that on one occasion a very tall man in black came in, turned the blouse and then slowly walked away again, but she did not say if this was the wraith of a prospective bridegroom. And perhaps she did not entertain the idea that the local lads might sometimes, out of mischief, decide to take part in this curious magical ritual. It ought to be said, however, to those who doubt, that rituals almost identical to these were practised in all parts of Britain. How, if they were absurd, how. if they had a high failure rate, were they so implicitly believed in for centuries over such a wide area?

At Hallowe'en, at midnight – that great witching hour – some girls would, while eating an apple, look in the mirror expecting to see their future husband gazing over their shoulder. Surely this too must have been an unnerving experience. As with all these rituals there must have been an initial sense of excitement, pleasure perhaps, which then gave way to a germ of uncertainty, a rising anxiety. It is impossible to believe that many girls had the will to see such rituals to their conclusion.

Another simpler form of divination, also carried out at Hallowe'en – one which was less likely to cause fear – was for a couple interested in each other to place two roasted chestnuts in front of the fire. As each of them thought of the other's name, the following words were repeated, the pronoun differing accordingly:

'If he loves me, pop and fly,
If he hates me, lie and deny.'

Another version has the last word as 'die'.

If the chestnuts burned steadily side by side, it was a favourable sign that they would marry and live happily ever afterwards. If either chestnut should burst or move away, then the love-match was doomed. So no fear this time, though perhaps there was disappointment enough.

Those participating had always to prepare themselves for bad as well as good news. Take the game – for it is likely that some regarded it less seriously than others – where everyone fastened an apple on a string and twirled it round in front of the fire. Happy the young person whose apple fell off first, for they had just been given a sign that they were about to be married. Imagine the excitement as the apples fell off, for this indicated the order in which the weddings would occur. And pity the last one, sadly doomed to single estate.

In Eastbourne in about 1915, 'we pulled each finger and the number of joints that cracked meant one had that number of sweethearts'. The consoling factor here was that if the result was disappointing perhaps another pull of the fingers on a later occasion might produce a more optimistic conclusion.

Some groups of girls relied on playing cards to work out their matrimonial futures. The cards were dealt and the girl who found the ace of diamonds was destined to wed a rich man. Alas for those who had been dealt the jack of clubs or spades for they faced a life of poverty and misery. The king of diamonds or hearts indicated a fair-haired husband while the king of clubs or spades offered a man with dark hair. To add to the failure of the promise of a rich and handsome husband, those given the jack of hearts or diamonds were shown to have an unknown enemy.

How long before marriage beckoned? That too could be revealed. A ring was suspended by a thread held steadily inside a glass tumbler. When it began to move, the number of times it struck the sides of the glass foretold the number of years which would pass before marriage. It could be a depressing occasion for those with unsteady hands.

Some went to witches who were supposed to have foreknowledge. At Bury, a wise-woman used to receive young men and women who would find out whether their husbands or wives would be short or tall, rich or poor, dark or fair.

And supposing a girl struck lucky and found her Mr Right. And yes, supposing the man, too, found his longed-for life-partner. And supposing that they were engaged to be married. Even then the course of true love might not run smoothly. Give a knife or a pair of scissors or anything sharp-edged to your lover and it would cut your love asunder, so they used to say, and the prospect of marriage would fly out of the window.

Nothing is certain in this world as far as even the most committed lovers are concerned. A Brighton beach photographer commented that some engaged couples refused to have their photographs taken on the grounds that if they did so, the engagement might be called off. Perhaps it was a fear of tempting fate, that anxiety that constantly runs through the whole business of superstition. 'Don't count your chickens,' we hear said time and again. 'Don't tempt Providence,' we are regularly told.

And incidentally and away for the moment from potential brides and grooms, let's stay with the idea of the reluctance to have a photograph taken. In 1939 a *Sussex County Magazine* article about gypsies written by a medical man included the following lines:

'To the present day they fear – or affect to fear – the taking of their photographs ... "No, doctor, I ain't going to have you take my photygraph no more. I've had nought but ill-luck since you took me last year," said a handsome old Romany woman.

' "I'm sorry for that," I said, "because I've got some packets of your favourite Nosegay baccy with me, that I meant to give you if ... "

' "Oh well, doctor," she hastened to add, "seeing as how it's you ... ' "

So, then, back again to the arrangements for the marriage and the calling of the banns. In the 1870s William Parish commented on the wariness of people going to church to hear them called. It was feared, he said, that the children of those who did so were in danger of being born deaf and dumb.

And now to the wedding and a hoped-for sunny day for this predicted future happiness.

In 1873 a witness observed: 'In Sussex I have seen wheat scattered over the bride and bridegroom as they left the church. No doubt rice, which seems to be becoming fashionable, is used with the same meaning as that attached to wheat. Its substitution for wheat is, probably, due to the fact that it is more easily obtained in an ordinary household.'

Wheat? Yes, associated with growth, prosperity, success – a genuine symbol which did stand for something in the way that little bits of coloured paper really represent nothing in particular save a vague sense of cheerfulness.

Now, pins. You may know the verse:

See a pin and pick it up
All the day you'll have good luck.

Perhaps that was why a bride, coming from the church in her wedding gown, was often mobbed by her unmarried female friends and had all of the pins on her dress taken. The belief was that whoever possessed one of them would be married within the year. Why the bride had so many pins about her garments is unclear. One possibility – and this is pure guesswork – is that the bride traditionally carried these good luck pins, knowing that they were likely to be in great demand.

Still, take warning. They are funny things, pins. They were often used in witchcraft. So heed the old words: 'A yellow, crooked pin must on no account be picked up, or the tidy person who removes it from the floor will die an old maid.'

And, by way of conclusion, they used to say that when parsley grows well in the garden you can tell who is the master in the house – the wife! William Parish added that rosemary would blossom only where 'the mistus' (the usual pronunciation of 'mistress') was master.

It always seems to be a good year for parsley and rosemary!

Mothers and Babies

So the wedding is over and the bride has had it whispered in her ear – as if she did not already know the truth of the matter – that a piece of the wedding cake must be saved.

'My grandmother told me,' said a Horsham woman in 1953, 'that unless a piece of wedding cake was saved for the first christening then it was a sure thing that the bride would be barren.'

But saving wedding cake or no, there was always an ample number of births. Just look at what Nature tells you: 'In 1950,' according to one correspondent in *Folklore* magazine, 'a vicar's wife of my acquaintance remarked to her charwoman that the number of births in the parish had been unusually large that year. The woman replied that this was only to be expected because there had been a very fine crop of nuts in the previous autumn. When questioned further, she could not explain the connection: she only knew that it was an accepted local sign and, in her experience, a true one.'

There was of course a long association with nutting and the Devil who was said to hang about the woodlands just waiting to catch the unwary. But there was also the old nudge and wink, well known in rural areas, about what young folk got up to when they went off with their nutting bags. Once down in the depths of the woods their minds were on other things. And Nature simply responded by producing an equally fine crop of nuts.

The birth of a child has always been surrounded by rituals designed to assure the young one's safe and happy future, but these used to be more exotic than now. So the first time the baby was taken from the room in which he was born – and 'she' is included here, just as in life the male embraces the female – he had to be carried upstairs before being carried down. But what if the child was on the top floor or in a single-storey house? In that case some other way of raising him had to be found. A ladder could be brought into the room. Or a piece of furniture could be stood upon, just enough to break any possibility of bad luck. Going up signified progress, growth, future success, a move towards the heavens, so climbing a flight of stairs or mounting a ladder could only make good fortune more likely.

It was considered that if left alone in the same room with a baby in a cradle, cats would creep in and suck its breath. Witches, feared as shape-shifters, were believed capable of assuming any form, including that of a cat. And in addition to witches who might curse the child there were fairies who might exchange one of their own weakly children for a healthy human baby. As a safeguard, therefore, round the cradle was placed a scattering of yarrow,

 a plant otherwise known as Old Man's Pepper. Of course, pepper deters. And we all know who the Old Man was.

Until they were baptised many babies, who as yet did not have the protection of God, were kept indoors. Only baptism could give absolute protection against the onslaughts of the wicked. But prior to baptism, there was always a reluctance to divulge a baby's name. It was almost as if the child were being protected from identity theft by the forces of evil. And further, on this matter of naming, as late as 1956 a witness in Eastbourne declared that it was unlucky to name a later child after one that had died. It would not live, she said.

And by the way, just a warning to mothers and their visitors, come to admire the new-born child:

'If you rock the cradle empty
Then you shall have babies plenty.'

Not all mothers wished for yet another child. After all, another mouth to feed was not always welcome in impoverished cottages. And the chances of dying in childbirth were high. A schoolmistress in a West Sussex parish was remembered for constantly telling her pupils not to touch the unoccupied cradle. She would snap at them, 'Leave that alone, can't ye? I have children enough already.'

As for the new mother there were also other matters requiring care. The churching of women was more regularly observed than today. Even so, there was always the uncertainty within the church over its significance. Was the first visit to church after giving birth to purify the mother after giving birth or was it to give thanks?

This uncertainty and its consequent controversy resulted in a range of sometimes superstitious interpretations. One of the most widespread of these was that a woman should not leave the house until the occasion when she went to be churched. Nor must she go into other houses. If she did either, she would bring bad luck, a common consequence of defying a taboo. Some believed that if an unchurched woman did go out, carrying her baby, she should not cross water. Others held the view that she should neither cross a main road nor even, on her way to church, look up at the sky.

The author Thomas Lupton, writing in 1660, confidently stated: 'If a man be the first that a woman meets after she comes out of the church, when she is newly churched, it signifies that her next child will be a boy; if she meets a woman, then a wench is likely to be her next child.'

The baptismal ceremony was not regarded simply as a welcoming into the Christian community but it also contained an element of exorcism, the expulsion of the Devil from the newborn child. The north door of churches – the so-called Devil's Doors – were left open on these occasions for the Devil to make his exit.

The following anecdote comes from Charlotte Latham: 'I was lately present at a christening in Sussex, when a lady of the party, who was a godmother of the child, whispered in a voice of anxiety. "The child never cried. Why did not the nurse rouse it up?" After we had left the church, she said to her, "Oh nurse, why did you not pinch baby?" and, when the baby's good behaviour was afterwards commented upon, she observed with a very serious air, "I wish that he had cried".'

Many babies were pinched at the font by their mothers and nurses in order to produce the right result. Care was also taken to ensure that the baptismal water was not be wiped off the baby's forehead.

Right through our lives the remnant of this belief about the rejection of the Devil continues when we say our little prayer, 'Bless you,' to the sneezer in the hope that whatever evil spirit might have crept in has now been successfully expelled. Nor is it simple politeness or the fear of spreading germs that causes us to place our hands across our mouths when we cough. We are barring entry to the Devil. In former times, for similar reasons, an adult hand would make the sign of the cross and close the mouth of a baby who coughed or yawned.

On a more homely note it was believed that a baby's cap must be left off for the first time on a Sunday. In that way it would not catch cold. As for cutting the baby's hair and nails, there were quite seriously observed rules. Hair and nail clippings were frequently destroyed, for witches could put them in the wax with which they were said to make effigies of their intended victims.

Particularly in Sussex it was believed that an infant's hair should be cut at the time of a waxing moon. To cut it when there was a waning moon could bring ill luck. And why waxing? Presumably because of its association with growth and progress. As for the child's nails, these were not to be cut before it was a year old. Otherwise it would become light-fingered. If the nails needed to be trimmed before the required age they were to be bitten short by the parent. As the verse went:

> *Monday for health,*
> *Tuesday for wealth,*
> *Wednesday the best day of all,*
> *Thursday for crosses,*
> *Friday for losses,*
> *And Saturday no luck at all.*
> *But a child whose nails on a Sunday are shorn*
> *Will live to wish he'd never been born.*

And so from the cradle the baby embarked on a life which would always have the shadowy thoughts of what might happen if he failed to observe the rituals, the observances, of so many generations.

Death, the Ever-Present Companion

Think of this. One of John Coker Egerton's parishioners at Burwash had been married for 15 years. His wife had been confined 11 times in addition to suffering several miscarriages. She had had 13 children, once three at a birth. Six were still alive, the eldest 14. Such figures, such sadnesses. In all, she must have been pregnant for about eight years and for the same amount of time, or perhaps even longer, in mourning.

Or take the Wilson family, living in Alfriston's High Street. The parents outlived all of their six children, none of whom lived beyond twenty-three years and three of whom, Ann (12), Mary (4) and Sally (11), died within eighteen months of each other in 1843 and 1844.

Down all the long years of past centuries there is a depressing toll of children, young boys and girls who never reach maturity. In the burial registers we read of the deaths of so many babies only days old. Somehow we can't imagine it, the loss, so regular, so feared. What griefs they bore, these fathers and mothers. What tragedies they must have anticipated, knowing the high chance of losing some of their babies. We wonder at the seeming injustice of it; we wonder how they could accommodate themselves to the loss of two, three, four of their little children. So very frail the threads of life at this time, constantly pregnant women constantly mourning the loss of their babies.

Most baptisms of working-class babies were performed on Sundays. However, high infant mortality, especially in the first few days, led many parents to have a sickly infant baptised immediately and at home.

But the horror of it all – this never failing presence of death. The burial register at Alfriston carries this chilling marginal note:

'13 July, 1832 Samuel Bussey aged 21.
Buried in the night without service having died of the small pox being in a dreadful state.'

'Buried in the night.' The grimmest corners of our past are illuminated by marginal notes like this. And speculation about who would go next must have been the uppermost thought in many minds. One of the long-lasting superstitions still holds. In 1984 a woman in Chichester said, 'When my father died and an old neighbour died, someone said to me: "There'll be another death soon. They always go in threes".' They must have gone in threes, fours and fives in our county's past.

Small wonder that in earlier centuries such omens of death were seen at every turn. With a life expectancy of 37 in the age of the first Queen Elizabeth and only 50 at the beginning of the First World War, death must have seemed omnipresent, heralded so often by inconsequential happenings which were taken as serious warnings. For some people certain sounds were sure announcements of imminent death.

After visiting friends, in January 1751, Walter Gale, the Mayfield schoolmaster, wrote in his diary: 'I told them in discourse that on Thursday last the town clock was heard to strike 3 in the afternoon twice, once before the chimes went, and a second time pretty near a ¼ of an hour after. The strikes at the 2nd striking seemed to sound very dull and mournfully; this, together with the crickets coming to the house at Laughton just at our coming away, I look upon to be sure presages of my sister's death.'

These insects turn up again in *The Years with Mother* by the prolific Victorian Sussex author Augustus Hare, who lived in Goring. A death in the family was imminent and Hare wrote, 'Our parting was very near. Lea called me downstairs to hear the extraordinary sound that was going on . . . it was as if hundreds of thousands of crickets were all chirping together. They appeared everywhere in swarms on the hearths downstairs. The noise was quite deafening; but they only came out that night, they were never heard before, and the next day they had totally disappeared.'

But there were all sorts of other sounds which had significance. 'In the village in Sussex in which I live,' a correspondent wrote in *Notes and Queries* in 1870, 'it is generally believed, at least by the female portion of the community, that if the church clock strikes twelve while a hymn is being sung in the morning service a death will follow in the week.' Note this, the reference to 'the female portion of the community.' Was the writer implying that only women could believe in such illogicalities.? Was he saying that men are above all of this nonsense? Well, he was a man of his time.

For some the funeral bell, if it sounded unduly heavy, was enough to suggest another early burial. In reply to her mistress's remark that there was to be another funeral that week, a servant responded, 'I told Jane, the day of old Master Smith's burial, that I knew from the sound of the bell that we should have another pretty soon.'

An unusual rattling of the church door indicated to some people that it would be open to receive another corpse before the week was out. But what was an unusual rattling? Come to that, exactly what sound was the funeral bell tolling that it gave such clear warning of another death?

But there were other strange local interpretations of quite ordinary matters. On one occasion a cook was talking to her mistress about the kitchen fire.

'It was indeed the blackest fire I ever saw,' she said, 'and though I am not superstitious I did not like its looks. We have had two sudden deaths close to us and if I do not make that horrid, black-looking fire blaze up, see if we don't soon hear of another death or else some terrible misfortune.' And this cook claimed not to be superstitious! Yet she might as well be claiming to have the power of life and death. All she had to do was poke the fire.

Some omens were quite beyond any understanding, such as dreaming about teeth, which was said to forecast a sorrow of some kind. Another bizarre omen came from a farmer's wife in the 1870s. She said that she had known three days earlier that a neighbour's death was near at hand. She had known it because the woman had longed for cider. But surely the dying sometimes do crave a drink. 'I do not think that had anything to do with it,' the farmer's wife replied to that reasonably expressed doubt, 'for it is considered a sure sign of death when such people long for it.'

There were so many innocent occurrences that our forefathers took to be sure signs of their mortality and of someone's impending death. Here is the nineteenth century naturalist, Richard Jefferies, observing that 'somewhere within doors, in the huge beams or woodwork, the death tick is sure to be heard in the silence of the night: even now the old folk listen with a lingering dread.'

Right down the years the eerie ticking sound of the little wood-burrowing death-watch beetle had been regarded with dread. Surely, it was thought, such a sound came as a warning and could only have some supernatural cause.

In November, 1870, John Coker Egerton recorded the death of a 71-year-old farm labourer who had died that morning after a short illness. On the same day he called on old Granny Watson. She was not surprised to hear the rector's news of the death. She told him that when she got up that morning she had put her foot through the heel of her stocking. 'She knew somebody would die soon,' Egerton tells us, 'and, sure enough, old Isaac was the one.'

So with death such a frequent visitor, it is hardly surprising that quite ordinary day-to-day occurrences took on the status of fearful warnings. There were always such omens, all sorts of little happenings threatening another passing. Death was always there. It was a never-failing topic of conversation. How could it be otherwise? Don't tempt Death. Don't invite him into the house. Don't think of putting elder wood on the fire, for surely the death of a family member will follow. 'Don't use a new broom in the house during the month of May,' an old gentleman reminded a servant girl. He remembered the old rhyme and its promise.

> *If you sweep the house with broom in May,*
> *You'll sweep the head of the house away.*

Odd that fresh-looking broom – the bush, that is – should be looked upon so unfavourably. Charlotte Latham, presumably in her capacity as vicar's wife, was visiting a girl who was dying from tuberculosis. She was surprised to find the patient in an agitated state about some spring flowers which had been placed on her bed. Was she worried about the smell, Mrs Latham asked her. Did she find it disagreeable? No, the girl replied, she found the smell very pleasant. 'But yet I should be very glad if you would throw away that piece of yellow broom,' she said, 'for they do say that death comes with it if it is brought into the house in blossom during the month of May.'

A flower regarded with equal dread was the snowdrop. A child who was scolded by her mother for bringing home a single snowdrop was told that 'it looked for all the world like a corpse in its shroud, and that it always kept itself quite close to the earth, seeming to belong more to the dead than to the living.'

The child's mother had no objection to a bunch of snowdrops. It was the single flower which had upset her.

As for primroses, they came by their surprisingly unfortunate reputation simply because they were often strewn on graves and also used to dress corpses in the coffin. In this way they became tarnished as omens of death.

Then there is a case of a woman who went visiting, carrying a piece of blossoming blackthorn. She never got inside the house before it was snatched from her and thrown outside. The householder said to her, 'How could you think, ma'am, of bringing that death token into my house?'

On 18th October, 1880, Egerton wrote in his diary of his dog howling quite suddenly. His servants unhesitatingly interpreted that as meaning someone had died. Such an interpretation might be just so much tosh to modern man but the servants' belief was later supported by the fact that someone had already died earlier that day in the village.

To so many Sussex men and women, these omens were no less than the grimmest warnings of inescapable fate. Bees, for example, could be relied upon to forecast a forthcoming death.

'Some years since,' Dr Martin of Pulborough informed *Notes and Queries* in 1851, 'the wife of a respectable cottager in my neighbourhood died in childbed. Calling on the widower soon after, I found that although deeply deploring an event which left him several motherless children, he spoke calmly of the fatal termination of the poor woman's illness as an inevitable and foregone conclusion. On being pressed for an explanation of these sentiments, I discovered that both he and his poor wife had been warned of the coming event by her going into the garden a fortnight before her confinement and discovering that their bees, in the act of swarming, had made the choice of a dead hedge stake for their settling place. This is generally considered as an infallible sign of a death in the family, and in her situation it is no wonder that the poor woman should take the warning to herself – affording, too, another example of how a prediction may assist in working out its own fulfilment.'

A note written by Reverend Henry Hoper, vicar of Portslade in the early part of the nineteenth century, indicates nevertheless that there always used to be some hope for the dying in his parish. He wrote: 'Singular superstition exists at Portslade and has been entertained within the memory of man, that a dying person can be recovered if thrice carried round and thrice bumped against a thorn of great antiquity, which stands on the down, ever ready to dispense its magic power to all believers.

'A few years ago a medical attendant gave up all hopes of his patient. The goodies of the village obtained the doctor's and sick man's consent to restore him to health, and having carried him round the tree, bumped the dying man and had the mortification of carrying him back a corpse.'

The 'goodies', Hoper seems to imply, were Portslade's superstitious busybodies, stuck in the past.

In the eighteenth century and lingering on into the nineteenth century, belief in such magic rituals was still very much alive even when the above example and others like it must have so frequently suggested that it was not wise to place one's trust in such a method of recovery. But hope so often triumphs over experience.

Inevitably, there were conventions associated with the death chamber. One woman who was present at a death said 'that as the poor gentleman's death struggles did not cease after she had left a passage for the spirit to go out by opening the door and window, she thought it might be the cabinets being locked that hindered.' So the cabinet doors were opened.

Another woman recalled her early days in service in Sompting in 1820 when she attended her dying mistress. 'Whilst the woman was dying I was standing at the foot of the bed when a woman desired me to remove, saying, "You should never stand at the foot of a bed when a person is dying." The reason I ascertained was because it would stop the spirit in his departure to the unknown world.'

In an age when there was little palliative medicine and when the final agonies of the dying could be eased only with difficulty, some died hard – but it is interesting to see what people sometimes attributed to a patient's lingering death. Pigeon or gamebird feathers in pillows or mattresses were often thought to prevent deaths occurring quickly, as the following instance, passed on by that tireless recorder, Charlotte Latham, demonstrates: 'The wife of a Sussex clergyman was told by a rural sick-nurse that never did she see anyone die so hard as old Master Short, and at last she thought (though her daughter said there were none) that there must be game feathers in the bed and she tried to pull it from under him, but he was a heavy man and she could not manage it alone and there was no-one with him but herself, so she got a rope and tied it round him, and pulled him off the bed, and he went off in a minute quite comfortable, just like a lamb.'

Yet another of Mrs Latham's confidants told her that there was a widely held belief about *rigor mortis*. If a corpse did not stiffen soon after death it was taken as a sure sign that another member of the family would soon die. 'The day after my master's death,' the informant said, 'one of his sisters-in-law came into the room and asked the nurse if she had ever heard that a limp corpse was a bad sign, and nurse made answer, "La, miss, it's nothing but an old woman's saying." But she winked at me and when miss was gone she said, "I didn't like to tell her the truth, but master's corpse not stiffening is a sure sign that death will be knocking pretty soon again at the door of this house for some other of the family".'

Corpses were routinely kept at home during the interval between death and burial, and various conventions and rituals had to be observed for reasons both practical and symbolic. In many homes, both in Sussex and throughout the country, a bowl of salt was placed on the corpse's breast as soon as possible after death and it stayed there until the body was placed in the coffin. One witness who saw this particular practice observed in an unnamed Sussex village wrote, 'I saw it down in this village a day or two ago, and was told that it was to prevent the corpse swelling.' Others have said that as salt was a preservative of meat, it might as a result have become connected with human corpses. Yet another explanation linked this convention to the exorcism service in which salt is used to keep the Devil at bay and to prevent him from seizing the souls of the departed.

There were further anxieties about the grave being dug and left open over a Sunday. It was another of those situations which was thought to lead to further deaths. One account says: 'An unusual number of deaths occurred in a small Sussex village last year, the last of which happened on a recent Saturday night. A villager thereupon presaged another death within the month, because the corpse would of necessity lie unburied over a Sunday, and she justified her prediction by referring to the last two deaths, the latter of which followed the earlier within a month, the earlier one also having lain over the Sunday.'

In 1944 a contributor to the *Sussex County Magazine* mentioned almost with a sense of despair that this old superstition was still firmly adhered to.

'It is an ominous sign if a corpse should be left unburied on Sunday, for this will mean that the death of another of the village community will occur before the week is out. I have frequently heard this strange idea expressed with utmost sincerity and with a genuine belief in the inevitability of such a correlation of events.'

There was a correct procedure to be carried out on the day of a funeral. The front door had to stay open after the corpse had left the house and it had to remain open until the burial was complete. Should this not be done, another death would follow. On the morning of a funeral at St Mary's Almshouses in Chichester, as soon as the body had been carried out, the dead woman's niece unthinkingly locked the door behind her. Immediately those inside started hammering on the door in an attempt to force it open.

'Hang that good for nothing woman!' one of them said. 'Her locking this door before the old girl is buried will bring death among us pretty soon again.'

In 1978 the *Sussex Express* tells of a practice still maintained in a house in mourning. During the absence of the funeral party somebody would change the furniture in the bedroom of the deceased so that if the ghost returned it would not recognise the place and would in consequence leave the family in peace.

A hundred years earlier an undertaker in Lavant told a contributor to *Notes and Queries* that 'the pins employed on a corpse for any purpose are never used again, but are always deposited in the coffin and buried with the dead body'. The same undertaker promised to stick half a dozen black pins in the gatepost of the meadow through which the funeral cortege passed. It seems that this was intended to protect the mourners who had carried or who had followed the coffin from any evil from the Devil that might befall them.

But to meet a funeral cortege was enough for some to turn tail immediately and return home, regardless how urgent a business matter was being abandoned. For such people passing a funeral was a sure sign that their own death would shortly follow.

And the next life? An old custom was employed in Alfriston and Falmer until the 1930s. Shepherds were buried with a piece of wool in their hand. After all, at the Last Judgement many things are to be taken into account, including the regularity of church attendance. Shepherds were busy folk, working seven days a week, unable to desert their flocks, but come Judgement Day the shepherds of Alfriston and Falmer would hold up their hands with their pieces of wool and their absences would be understood and they would be forgiven. Well, at least this was a hopeful sign.

All these notions, all this relentless accumulation of superstitions: it was almost impossible not to come across some sign of impending death and disaster in the course of the day. It really does seem that our forefathers were indiscriminate hoarders of long outdated notions. Did they really believe each and every promised threat to their lives and the lives of their relatives and friends? Or did they prune them down?

It is not clear if these beliefs were accepted in their entirety in each and every household, village or town. Indeed, it is difficult to think that they were.

On the other hand, even to accept but a minority of such superstitions would be enough to cloud the lives of many folk for many a day.

Down to the Sea

The naturalist and writer, Richard Jefferies, described the Brighton fishermen of the mid- to late-nineteenth century as 'quite separate and belonging to another race.'

Quite right. And these words could well have applied to every fishing community in the British Isles. Fishermen had always been quite separate from the rest of the inhabitants of their town or village, perhaps able to share their lives only with those who could comprehend the hazardous daily enterprise in which they were involved. There is a sense that they were a caste apart, a different breed of men, not as the rest of us.

The fishing community, along with the miners, was one of the last to give up its superstitious beliefs and the last of the true believers probably quit this world in the 1970s. They went to their work each day conscious of the uncertainties they faced, hoping to ensure their safety with a range of rituals, most of which were foreign to those working on land. Whilst they shared all of the superstitions held by the landsmen in their localities, there were always beliefs peculiar to fishing folk, unique to their way of life and their arduous trade. It is said that the traditional seaman wore gold earrings because he believed that it would help his eyesight. But it is more likely that he saw it as his insurance policy. They would pay his fare home were he stranded. And they would in the worst case help pay for his funeral.

One of the most important principles of superstition is that beginnings set the pattern of good or bad fortune for the future. The notion that Friday is the unluckiest day of the week is widespread throughout the British Isles and not solely in the fishing community. Perhaps there is some truth in the idea of which Charlotte Latham reminds us: 'Adam and Eve ate the forbidden fruit on a Friday.' Others have referred to it as the day on which Christ's blood was shed. For whatever reason, this wariness about Friday goes back at least to medieval times. Our Sussex seamen would not – will not, even today – use a new net on this day. Perhaps they would not even go to sea on a Friday if none of their old nets was serviceable. Does that sound odd? Well, some people refuse to move house on a Friday, although it ought to be a convenient day for them to do so.

As for embarking on a new kind of fishing – say, changing from catching lobsters to fishing with lines – there was no possibility of this venture commencing on a Friday, for who knows what disaster might befall anyone daring to flout such tradition. People who had taken such risks had ended up with their boats wrecked or the whole crew drowned.

Here is Ted Watherington, a Brighton fisherman, talking in the 1980s. 'You wouldn't go to sea if there'd been a gale of wind for a couple of weeks and you couldn't get off, and all of a sudden Thursday it would come a bit fine, and Friday it would be nice and beautiful and calm, so that you could go to sea. They wouldn't go to sea on a Friday. Unlucky. If you had been off for the sake of the weather, and all of a sudden it had become calm on a Friday, you wouldn't take your boat out to sea on that Friday.'

Even if he was out of work for a fortnight and doubtless needing to earn, nothing would induce Ted to start on a Friday. Johnny Humphrey, another member of an old Brighton fishing family, backs this up.

'And another thing,' Johnny says, 'they would never start a season on a Friday. It could blow hard, say we got our nets ready on the Monday, and it blowed hard all the week, and it come fine on Friday, they wouldn't go and start their season on a Friday. It was just unlucky. It could blow for another week, still wouldn't go on a Friday.'

In the fishing communities in and around Hastings there was another dreaded day as the *Hastings and St Leonards Observer* tells us: 'There are fishermen who dread the 9th March, and one of these, an owner, ever since the terrific storm of that date five years ago, positively refuses either to go to sea himself or to allow his boat to be away on that unlucky day.' Three Hastings men had drowned on that day in 1891, two boats had been lost and another seven damaged.

But back to beginnings – it was thought (and still is) that if it was fine at midnight on New Year's Eve that was a good augury for the rest of the year's fishing. On the other hand, if it was not fine, that suggested a bad year to come. The beginning of any enterprise was seen to determine whatever good or bad fortune was to follow.

When a new boat was commissioned the utmost care was taken that there should be no chance of encouraging bad luck. Of course, no-one would ever dream of having a boat painted green. With all its connotations of sickness and immaturity, green was always unlucky. Some are said to have associated it with the colour worn by fairies and nobody would wish to upset *them*. As for green sea boots, they were – and are – totally out of the question.

Wherever possible the number 13 was avoided, although there is some evidence that our anxieties about Friday 13th do not to go back before Victorian times. Be that as it may, you will only very rarely find a boat with the registered number 13. Some boat owners have even resisted a number where the digits add up to 13.

Arthur Ransom, son of one of the founders of Hastings boatbuilders Ransom and Ridley, left an interesting account of the launching of a new vessel. 'The jacks were under her and the men were in the rigging to shake her and give her the initial motion, but she would not stir. Presently, a black retriever was discovered on board. The poor creature was well tarred and chivvied away. The vessel slipped gallantly into the water at once. That afternoon, a reputed witch living in a house I knew well, made her way home covered with tar.'

Ransom was sure this story was true because he heard it from the son of the woman who washed the tar from the witch.

At another launching in 1805, a very large craft could not be got down into the water. There was a large crowd of four thousand. It was concluded that a witch, an old woman called Margaret Bourner, was responsible. Apparently she had told her neighbours that the boat 'wouldn't go that day' but she assured them that it would go on the following morning, and so it did. But nobody seems to have challenged her to demand that the boat be allowed off its moorings. Perhaps they did not dare. After all, what might befall those sailing in her?

Fishermen in Sussex and, indeed, in many other parts of the country believed that holed stones, known also in the county as hag stones or lucky stones, brought good fortune and gave protection to those carrying them. It is said that few fishing boats made their way out to sea without such a stone fixed by a piece of copper wire somewhere in the woodwork. How else would the crewmen be saved from drowning or the boat from capsizing? These are the selfsame stones which used to be placed in houses and barns as a protection against witches, fairies and bad neighbours.

Another way of what really seems like propitiating the sea gods was to place a coin in a dann (buoy). It was just a little gift, just to acknowledge and perhaps pacify those powers that seamen could not control.

Before the start of the mackerel season at the end of April, Brighton fishermen used to decorate the masts of their little boats with garlands of flowers. On the shingly beach, bread and cheese was distributed to children who wished the boats good luck. This latter point, this wishing good luck, is interesting and will be returned to later.

So then, the boat readied, the crewmen would leave for the fishing grounds. Interesting that in a rocking, pitching, cramped little craft there was time always to follow the appropriate ceremonies which so often included a prayer.

When casting drift nets in the mackerel and herring seasons the fishermen observed the following ritual: as each barrel (which was attached to every two nets out of the 120 usually cast out) was cast overboard, the crew would cry:

Watch, barrel, watch! Mackerel [or herring] for to catch,
White they may be, like a blossom of a tree,
God send thousands, one, two, and three,
Some by their heads, some by their tails,
God sends thousands, and never fails.

Once the last net was overboard the skipper called out: 'Seas all!' How similar this verse is to the wassailing songs sung in the countryside in the expectation of a good harvest. Sometimes a yet more elaborate ritual was employed, beginning with the skipper's instruction:

'Now, men, hats off! God Almighty send us a blessing through Jesus Christ. Amen.'

Then each of the crew, perhaps of eight men, called out his own line:

First man: *Watch barrel! Watch! Mackerel for catch.*
Second man: *White may they be, like a blossom.*
Third man: *Some by head.*
Fourth man: *Some by tail.*
Fifth man: *May God send us mackerel! May he never fail.*
Sixth man: *Some by nose.*
Seventh man: *Some by the fin.*
Eighth man: *May God send as many as we can lift.*

Was this a genuine prayer? Or was it simply routine, a habit? That seems unlikely. Even today fishermen like Alan Hayes of Brighton say a prayer before casting their mackerel or herring drift nets. And when they catch a king herring or red herring — that is, a herring with very pronounced red fins and which acts as pilot of the shoal – it is dropped down the rudder trunk for good luck. Just to make sure. Just in case. But as with many of these superstitions, there is another version in which, for good luck, the fish is thrown back into the sea where it can resume its duties as pilot.

What runs through the DNA of our superstitions is a whole range of do's and don'ts and, in the case of fishermen, what may be done or said before even setting off to sea – and high on the list is the awareness that you must not tempt fate. Do that, just even suggest that something really good is going to occur, and you are tempting fate. In general terms we advise others not to count their chickens before they are hatched; we suggest that they should not be smug about their future prospects; we remind them that pride comes before a fall. And our fishermen throughout these islands, and indeed throughout the world, have a similar caution. They know that dawn with its clear blue skies can be deceptive, disastrously so. As a result, fishermen must never be wished 'Good luck' prior to setting out to the fishing grounds, a prohibition followed right round our coasts from Orkney to Cornwall. To break this taboo with such a greeting might lead to the abandonment of the day's fishing.

And there are other taboos. Even today, a fisherman does not promise those on land anything regarding his catch. No, he will not promise to a fish merchant so much cod or haddock or mackerel. That would almost guarantee a bad catch. It would be presumptuous to promise anything of that kind. And until it is landed, he will not even count his catch.

There are some other quite odd language taboos, words which fishermen refrain from using at sea or while engaged on land in other important aspects of their trade. These taboo words vary from place to place. Where Yorkshire fishermen or those at Plymouth or Lowestoft will not utter the word 'pig' lest it bring them bad luck, in Sussex the dread word is 'rabbits'.

Ted Watherington was in no doubt about that. 'You had to call them Bexhill Runners,' he explained. In other parts of the country the words 'hare', 'church' or 'egg', if used by anyone aboard, could lead to the abandonment of a day at sea.

At times, when there were difficulties on the boat, some might suggest that somehow a rabbit had been on board. This wariness of rabbits extended as far as seeing them on land. It was a very uncertain fisherman who went onto his boat having just seen one earlier. Oddly, meeting nuns on the way to the boat had the same effect. The story is told of the Brighton fisherman, Ted Gillam, taking a bus to Shoreham where his boat was docked. Part way through the journey two nuns boarded the bus. That made up his mind. Meeting nuns: it was a bad start, a warning no less, and there'd be no fishing that day. He got off the bus and went home.

This particular superstition extends to other fishing communities, but how can it be explained? Eastbourne fishermen had the same reaction on seeing a vicar on a Friday, and they thought that to meet a cross-eyed person was unlucky, especially if it was a woman. This particular anxiety was common in many parts of the country and some countered ill-effects of such meetings by spitting or crossing their fingers. Perhaps it is unnecessary to add that women, cross-eyed or not, were not allowed on board boats.

On board and at sea, the tiny bobbing craft was a world in itself with its own sensible, strict rules about safety, but also its superstitions which are so difficult to understand. For instance, no whistling was allowed on a boat. Should anyone whistle the boat could be turned round and returned home, another day's catch lost.

'Oh, you mustn't whistle, no, you whistle up the wind, they always told you that, you whistle up the wind,' Ted Gillam explained.

Frequently mentioned by fishermen was the hatch cover which, if taken off, had not to be placed upside down. This may be similar to the attitudes towards bowls and buckets when they are upside down, for these are suggestive of an upturned vessel, symbols of a stricken boat. Anything to do with water had to be carefully controlled. It is, even today, regarded as bad luck to lose a bucket overboard, and it is easy to understand the curious reasoning about why it was regarded as unlucky to sit on an upturned bucket.

And how did the fishermen respond to a succession of bad catches? If things were going seriously wrong it was time to burn the Devil out of the boat, time for a crew member to go round the boat with a burning torch, not of course to do damage but to rid it symbolically of 'Old Nick'.

But what about the embargo on white-handled knives, certainly not acceptable, either on board or ashore while net mending? It was a strange restriction but, like many superstitions, it defies explanation. Alan Hayes recalls the old fishermen in the 1950s, standing outside the arches on Brighton seafront, mending their nets.

'Every one of them would tell you they wouldn't use a white-handled knife. Absolutely not. It would bring them bad luck, you see.' Even so, Alan cannot say what was the origin of this curious belief. 'I've no idea,' he says, 'and I don't imagine any one of those old fellers could explain it either.' And again a variation – fishermen in Eastbourne would not use a new knife.

Safety is of major importance at sea. A slip on deck can have the most disastrous consequences. Yet the fish scales of herring were not washed off a boat's decks or off the fishermen's boots, presumably because that would be seen as a kind of rejection, a washing-away of their living, as if they had no need of the fish. In a similar fashion, many wives would not wash clothing on the day their husbands went to sea, for that too might be another symbolic washing-away which might lead to disaster.

It seems an intractable rule that the boat must not turn against the sun's course. It must always go 'sunwise' (clockwise) even if this presents problems. In past times, if fishermen inadvertently turned their boat in opposition to the direction of the sun, they would fear that they were in imminent danger. So even today boats at sea will generally turn 'sunwise'; so ropes are coiled on deck 'sunwise'; so nets are always put on this, the starboard side.

As for night-fishing, Brighton fishermen had a superstition about what they called the moon line, the moon's reflection on the surface of the water. The power of the moon had such an effect on so many aspects of life in times past, and at sea it would surely bring ill luck if the boat passed over the line.

These sometimes obscure superstitions, often only half-believed but still rigorously followed by many fishermen, are the inevitable consequences of a life spent each day in the eye of danger, facing hazards impossible to anticipate. Fishermen were always deeply aware of luck, both good and bad, but always unreliable. It was through their sometimes bizarre rituals and prohibitions that they strove to control their destinies. It is this that lies behind the superstitions observed by those who earned their living in such a precarious fashion.

Some Creatures Great and Small

In the following pages some of the many superstitions connected with animals, birds and insects are described. This is not by any means an attempt to cover the whole ground, for this would take a book in itself. Sufficient to say that other creatures, unmentioned here, were believed to possess powers which could work for or against humans.

Let's start with butterflies which we might expect would be highly regarded. They don't pester us as flies so often do; they don't sting; they look beautiful. The general view in several parts of the country is that they can bring us good luck and to ensure that they do so it is recommended that we follow the advice recorded in Sussex by E.V. Lucas at the beginning of the twentieth century:

The first butterfly you see,
Cut off his head across your knee,
Bury her head under a stone,
And a lot of money will be your own.

The same recommendation applies to Sussex snakes and in some areas of England to wasps. Unlike the butterfly, neither of these creatures guarantees money but both offer power over one's enemies.

Bees seem to be the aristocrats of the insect world. They are recorded as being highly regarded in the Ancient World, in Egypt, Greece and Rome as well as in other parts of Europe. Perhaps it was that they provided the gods with their sacred mead. There were also other ideas which connected them with both the gods and with the human soul.

Some regarded them as the winged messengers of the gods who carried news of the imminent arrival of a newcomer to the spirit world. Others saw them not as messengers but as the soul itself. It is doubtful if our Sussex forefathers saw them in either of the above capacities, but they seem to have had a greater reverence for the bee than for any other animal, bird or insect.

The most widespread story of bees is that they had always to be kept

 up-to-date with any news concerning the beekeeper and his family. Any major change affecting the keeper's family had to be conveyed to them with the teller first tapping gently on each hive with the house key. Then he would whisper the news to them in as respectful a fashion as possible. This telling of the bees has been recorded over centuries in Germany, France, the United States and in most counties of the British Isles. It was not necessarily the keeper who brought important news to the bees. In Kipling's *Puck of Pook's Hill* we learn that:

A maiden in her glory,
Upon her wedding day,
Must tell her bees the story,
Or else they'll fly away.

And this introduces an important factor in bee lore: that bees were extraordinarily sensitive and were easily affronted when not treated as true family members. Any neglect of these niceties and the bees would leave or, according to some authorities, would simply dwindle and die. Bees knew what was going on in the world of humans and, in their regal manner, would not stay with a family which quarrelled or swore. And note, incidentally, the use of the word 'keeper' in the text, for it does seem almost a matter of lèse majesté to use the word 'owner' when writing about bees.

So on the occasion of important family events, such as weddings, some keepers decorated the hives and even offered these significant family members some of the wedding breakfast. At other times, there were some keepers who even read letters to the bees from absent family members.

In their lordly fashion bees appear to have resented being bought or sold like domestic animals. According to E V Lucas:

If you wish your bees to thrive
Gold must be paid for every hive;
For when they are bought with other money
There will be neither swarm nor honey.

These, then, were a classy insect. They were not as other common-or-garden flying creatures. They would not be given away or sold to another keeper as if they were some article of crude commerce, an item of little worth. If they were to change hands there ought to be some suggestion that they were one side of an exchange of gifts. So someone was presented with a swarm of bees in return for, say, a piglet or a sack of corn. But the bees themselves disliked the thought of being part of some sordid little commercial transaction which neglected to acknowledge their true worth, and they had to be informed of any change of owner. It was only right.

When there was a death, as members of the family, the bees were to be told. In Sussex there was the belief that if a piece of black crepe was not put round each hive on such occasions the bees would die. And after the funeral some of the food and drink provided for mourners would be given to them. In the late nineteenth century a Sussex woman told a neighbour that her baby daughter had died after a few days because she had forgotten to tell the bees of her birth.

The behaviour of bees was regarded as a useful indicator of future events. Richard Jefferies, writing in 1879, commented: 'There is a superstition that if a humble-bee buzzes in at the window of the sitting room it is a sure sign of a coming visitor.'

Some people noted where bees settled, judging the location lucky or not, depending on the chosen place. As is indicated elsewhere in this book, it was thought to be a death omen if a swarm settled on a dead branch, especially near a dwelling house. Were bees to nest in the roof of a house it betokened that none of the daughters of the house would marry. Others interpreted that this warned of a house fire.

Certain birds were regarded as lucky and in consequence generally protected from molestation. They are celebrated in the following lines.

> *Robins and wrens*
> *Art God Almighty's friend;*
> *Martins and swallers,*
> *Are God Almighty's scholars*

There was no obvious reason to arrive at this conclusion about martins and swallows: rhyme rather than reason seems to have conquered here.

The most favoured of these birds was the robin, whose breast was bloodied at the crucifixion by Christ's crown of thorns. Illogically, the wren was always thought of as female and the wife of the robin.

In Greek mythology the wren was the king of the birds, and in Britain the Druids hailed it as the bird of prophecy. As such it was untouchable and there were dire consequences for those who harmed it. Yet there grew up a barbaric custom in this county as elsewhere in the British Isles: every St Stephen's Day (December 26) hedgerows were beaten by men and boys until one of the birds was caught and killed. Its body was stuck on the top of a pole. After the trophy had been paraded, its feathers were given to householders as a protection against witchcraft. The origin of this custom was the story that a wren had alerted the guards when Saint Stephen, the first Christian martyr, tried unsuccessfully to escape imprisonment.

By 1875 William Parish seems satisfied that at least in his county these birds were no longer in danger. 'The Sussex small boys have a Small Birds Act of their own,' he wrote, 'which is found sufficient for the protection of all birds which they consider entitled to protection, and commands much more respect and obedience than a recent Act of Parliament.'

And there was the lingering superstition that any who broke the code by robbing their nests would suffer a crooked finger. Elsewhere was the threat of a pimply face or even a broken arm for any such infraction.

Some birds were less highly favoured. There was, for example, an almost universal dislike of crows and ravens because of their hoarse croaking, which was regarded as ominous. Charlotte Latham writes of someone having 'a perfect faith that the thrice repeated caws of a carrion crow are a token of death'. An old woman living near Chichester, after hearing a raven croak, was said to have gone to bed for several days fully expecting to die even though, up till the time she heard the bird, she had been in good health. In another case a man walked into the house and announced to his family that they had lost a near relation. How did he know? Sure sign, he said, a carrion crow had just told him so by flying over his head and uttering three dismal caws.

There was a legend attached to the Campbell family at Aldwick. Whenever a male member of the family was about to die three ravens were said to appear on the walls of the castle. In 1934, when Sir Duncan Campbell was ill at Aldwick, a neighbour said that he had seen 'three miserable looking, drenched ravens' on the roof. Sir Duncan died shortly after.

As for magpies, the following verse is still recited today:

One is for sorrow, two for mirth,
Three for a wedding, four for a birth.

Quite a mixed reputation really. A single magpie on the left was seen as a certain sign of impending trouble and avoiding action had to be taken. In these circumstances, 'people of every class' took off their hats and bowed. When Mrs Latham enquired about this belief she was told that it was a bad bird 'and knew more than it should do, and was always looking about and prying into other people's affairs.' Still, this conscientious chronicler also found out that a tree with a magpie's nest in it was never known to fall. But whilst a magpie perching on the roof of a house was regarded as a good sign, proof of that house being in no danger of falling, seeing it on the back of an animal meant that it had sensed disease.

The barn or screech owl, often seen as a bird of ill omen, a herald of death, was another of those birds capable of causing great fear and anxiety. To some people, with its blood chilling shriek, it was not an earthly bird but rather something from some other unnamed, terrifying place. A servant sent one evening on an errand was absent for a long time. When she returned she explained the delay, saying that the Puck-bird was flying in front of her and she did not dare cross its path. But note how she called it: the Puck-bird, a name which conjured up ideas of wickedness, for Puck was not always a kindly fairy.

The cuckoo was another bird to which quaint stories were attached. On hearing the first cuckoo in spring, anyone with money in his pocket should not fail to turn it for otherwise he would be poor for the rest of the year. Others believed that whatever a person was doing when hearing the cuckoo's first call would be his principal occupation or interest for the rest of the year. Not as absurd as it may seem for, after all, most people are likely to hear the bird in working hours. Others worked out, from counting the number of calls, how long it would be until they either married or died.

One legend attaches to Heathfield where, each year in the spring, an old woman of uncertain temperament, put in an appearance. She, so it was believed, was in charge of all the cuckoos and she filled her apron with the birds. Then, if she were in a good temper, she released several. But if the fancy took her, if she was for some or other reason displeased, then she would release only one or two. Mrs Latham described how a woman in Fittleworth complained to her one spring about the cuckoo-keeper's bad temper. Apparently she had released only one cuckoo that year and, according to the woman, 'that 'ere bird is nothing to call a singer.'

Not that the Sussex children's song indicated their dissatisfaction with the bird:

The cuckoo's a merry bird: sings as she flies;
She brings us good tidings, and tells us no lies.
She picks up the dirt in the spring of the year,
And sucks little bird's eggs, to make her voice clear.

There is no suggestion here of any suspicion that the Jekyll and Hyde-like cuckoo changed at certain times into a hawk, though it was held to do so in some quarters.

Of birds in general there were several superstitions believed extensively throughout much of the country. For instance care must be taken over the disposal of hair. If birds were to find a strand of hair and put it in the nest the result would be severe headaches. And of course, there was a parallel threat of a witch obtaining anyone's hair, for this too could be used in even more devastating spells.

There was further danger if eggshells were not broken through after eating, because witches could put to sea in them. Indeed there were warnings not to bring blown birds' eggs into the house, for bad luck would inevitably follow. In consequence, in the spring, collections of eggs, often stolen from nests, were strung up but only in outhouses.

There was some small consolation for some victims fouled by a bird. They could account the mess on their clothing as a sign of future good luck. Others, holding to the belief that bird-fouling foretold bad luck, were doubly unfortunate.

A wild bird inside the house was largely considered a sign of misfortune as was a bird heard pecking at the window sill or fluttering against the window pane. Both of these were widely regarded as an ill omen. If there were a sick person in the house it could be taken as a sign that they would soon die.

In the old times, the shrew mouse had a distinctly mixed press in Sussex. For some reason or other it was considered as an evil omen. It was thought to be capable of laming people and responsible for poisoning cattle. One farmer was recorded as saying to his cattleman, 'Don't turn  those cows into that meadow or some harm will come to them for the field's full of those pick-nosed mice.' Fortunately, in the eyes of our predecessors the shrew was thought unable to cross any path or road trodden by man. When it did so, it was immediately struck dead. This was why, it was believed, so many were found lying dead on footpaths on the edge of fields without any wound or other apparent cause of death.

But despite the threat it was thought to pose, the shrew mouse was also believed to possess quite magical properties. A witness writing in the 1930s tells of a farmer in his eighties who was 'as superstitious as an African tribesman. He believed that to prevent the onset of rheumatism all one had to do was to carry a dead shrew in one's pocket.'

Another apparent cure for ailments afflicting people or their animals, was, with some crude ceremony, to bury a live shrew in the ground with a hole bored in it. At which point it may be pertinent to introduce another useful cure, this time from the mole.

'Does anyone remember Tom Weller, peg-legged cattle-tender on Ditchling Common?' a correspondent writes to the *Sussex Express* in 1972. 'He sold moles' feet in pairs which worn around the neck would cure the toothache.'

We can assume that Mr Weller was selling his wares – only the hind legs, by the way – perhaps within the memory of the correspondent and even in the lifetime of some of today's older readers. It seems reasonable to believe that he thought it worthwhile to spend his time awaiting purchasers and equally safe to assume that those who bought from him fully expected some positive results from wearing a charm-necklace of mole's legs, though some – and perhaps not surprisingly – preferred to carry a shrew mouse in their pockets.

It was generally held that meeting a hare was a very bad omen though some were less concerned if the animal appeared on the right rather than the left. Others would feel no anxiety provided it did not cross their path. It was all tied up with the idea that witches could turn themselves into hares.

Not unnaturally, cats and dogs gave rise to superstitions. If, for example, a stray dog or black cat, arrived at a house unannounced it brought good fortune with it. But supposing the cat suddenly became restless, longing perhaps to go back to its old home; suppose that it tried to escape: would the good luck go with it? Advice was always at hand. In this case the new owner was advised to put the cat in a cold oven for a few hours. This would wipe out all the cat's yearnings for its previous home and it would settle down happily and for ever with its new owner.

Now to another death omen. A blacksmith's wife at Ashington announced one day, 'I shall hear bad news before the day is over for late last night, as I was sitting up waiting for my husband who had gone to Horsham, what should I see on looking out of the window, lying close under it, but a thing like a duck, yet a great deal whiter than it ought to have been, whiter than any snow. I was all a-tremble and cried out quite loud, and off went the thing, faster than I ever saw anything run before.'

It was suggested that it might have been a neighbour's cat which looked whiter in the moonlight. The reply was, 'Oh dear, no. It was no cat nor anything alive.' She went on to say these white things were sent as warnings of a death and although she had received no sad news that night she remained convinced that a warning of some kind had been sent supernaturally.

As for beasts of the field, shepherds welcomed one black sheep in the flock as a good sign but two or three were bad.

There was an old superstition that at midnight on Christmas Eve or on St John's Eve (June 23) cattle lowed and knelt in acknowledgement of the births of Christ and St John the Baptist. In Sussex, unlike other places, there was no suggestion that they were endowed with the gift of speech on these occasions.

Neither horses, sheep or cattle ever seem to have offered any kind of threat to humans. Nevertheless, perhaps in an essentially agricultural community it was not surprising that interpretations of the movements and habits of many other creatures led to a range of superstitious belief.

More 'Oudacious' Creatures

We shall come to the dragons of Sussex legend very shortly but first we ought to dwell a while on their junior relative, the adder. In the eighth century the Anglo-Saxon Chronicle says: 'Wondrous adders were to be seen in the land of the South Saxons.' In what way these were 'wondrous' is not explained, but it may be assumed that they were especially impressive and that those folk with access to the ear of some or other recording monk told the tale of how fearsome and dangerous the creatures were.

Eleven centuries later a not dissimilar tale of an adder reached Charlotte Latham. One of her many informants told her that 'in the past year an oudacious large one' was said to be in the neighbourhood of Fittleworth. Apparently it was living near a footpath and would not permit anyone to pass. It would rush out, so Mrs Latham was told, and drive back with a terrible hissing and very bad smell any luckless person wandering by.

Another 'wondrous' adder, then? Without doubt country folk would know an adder when they saw one, but this particular creature does seem to have been acting out of character. And the smell? Some exaggeration perhaps?

In the Sussex of long ago there was no hesitation in deciding how to treat snakes. The universal belief was that they should be killed. If you were to kill the first snake you saw you would have power over your enemies for the rest of the year. (Of course, if one's enemies were to follow the same piece of advice there might be some confusion.)

Anyway, confusion or not, a snake, even were it cut in two, could not die until sunset. That's what was said. And don't earthworms appear to continue living after being chopped in two? Perhaps not until sunset, but certainly for some time after their being bisected.

Nevertheless, frightening and dangerous as they were held to be, there was some faith in the curative and magical properties of snakes. For example, they were used to cure goitre. It is recorded that at Withyham in 1851 the chosen method was to draw a snake three times three across the swelling – note the poetic, magical term, 'three times three' – and then put it in a tightly corked bottle which was buried. The swelling was expected to disappear as the snake slowly died.

Old Dame Jackson, a charmer living at West Chiltington used to buy adders for a penny each from anyone who brought them to her. She would boil them up and then it was simply a matter of bottling the oil which she used to cure earache, toothache, bellyache and rheumatism.

The antiquarian John Aubrey, writing in the early eighteenth century about snake skins, mentions that 'the Sussexians doe wear them for Hatt-bands, wch they say doe preserve them from the gripeing of the Guttes'.

As for people with severe difficulties of the digestive system, perhaps the result of parasitic worms, they were said to have 'a snake in the stomach'. One woman told Mrs Latham that snakes – 'nanny wipers' she called them – were fond of milk, and she had actually attempted a cure recommended to her. She had kept milk in her mouth and hoped that when the snake 'came quite up in her throat after it' she would be able to catch it, but this stratagem had failed. The woman was now convinced that there was only one way to catch a 'nanny-wiper'. First of all, a saucer of warm milk should be placed on the table, she said. Then the sufferer, sitting in a chair, should feign sleep, keeping the mouth wide open. When the 'nanny wiper' came out for the milk, the sufferer or an accomplice ought to kill it with a blow. Presumably this required the snake to be pulled out of the patient's mouth prior to its being hit.

As for those who did not suffer from goitre, various aches, 'gripeing of the Guttes' or 'snakes in the stomach', they could hang the snake skin in the house in the hope that they would have good luck.

But enough of snakes and adders! Let's get on to serpents. They would lead us to untold riches, so it was said.

There used to be buried treasure in several places in Sussex – at least, according to some old accounts. They were certain, those people in the past, that there was great wealth buried somewhere under The Mount at Pulborough, but it was never found. Nor was that at The Trundle near Goodwood, nor at Mount Caburn. There was more treasure in a wood at Fittleworth, too, apparently guarded by a ditch-dwelling spirit, and Clayton Hill also had its buried treasure. At Offington Hall, the old seat of the Delaware family, a blocked-up passage, approached only from the cellars, was believed to lead to treasure buried on Cissbury Hill. In the early nineteenth century some treasure hunters were offered half the riches found there if they would clear out the passage. But, according to the story, the diggers were confronted by several fearsome serpents and fled. Perhaps this was the owners' bluff, an attempt to dissuade illegal visitors from coming onto the property.

However, these serpents of myth, legend and tall-tale tellers, were not the first nightmare creatures to enter the mythology of the county. If there were tales circulating from Saxon times, presumably similar though long forgotten tales were going the rounds in the days of the Romans and of those who preceded them. The dragon, the serpent, the underwater monster, all had their indisputable place in the imagination of our ancestors, and reports of their deeds have travelled down the centuries and are lodged in our minds, too. We know them now through  fairy story, legend, myth, tales of knightly triumph, of rustic cunning, of courage rewarded. There must have been a time when they were not simply stories told at bedtime or by the fireside, but real living, chilling, history.

Take St Leonard, a sixth century French hermit who, for no discernible reason, had taken up his lonely abode in the forest that now bears his name. Not that there is historical proof that the saint ever made it to this part of the world, but legend has it that he did – that he loved it for the peace that allowed him to pray and contemplate the livelong day. And then his peace was disturbed. It was as if the neighbour from hell had arrived: a dragon, green and scaly overall, with a powerful wingspan and the ability to terrify the neighbourhood for miles around. And the saint, a soldier-holy man as it turned out, a man given to calm and peace for his prayerful life, was much put out by the intruder and took up arms to rid the world of this disturber of his peace.

Blood was spilled across the forest floor, the blood of the dragon and the blood of the saint. It was, it may be assumed, an epic struggle, fierce and protracted enough to remind us of Perseus and the Medusa, of Beowulf and Grendel and the mother of Grendel, and, of course, of St George and his dragon. Finally the saint prevailed, bruised and bloodied, his struggle commemorated by 'the prettiest relic of Sussex legendary lore', the lilies of the valley which sprang up wherever his blood had fallen. Here, in response to his prayers, peace and quiet were restored, even the song of nightingales stilled and the venom of the adder drawn. According to the legend, the snakes were also deprived of their hearing, which is why their bellies are inscribed:

If I could hear as well as see,
No mortal man should master me.

There is another story, its origins probably very ancient, which as ever has been subject to later storytellers' trimmings. It was over at Lymington, near Arundel, that the county's fiercest creature made his appearance, swooping over the neighbourhood for miles around and given to wrapping himself around his prey, carrying them off to the Arun swamplands before gobbling them up. So down its gullet went men, women, children as well as oxen, pigs, horses and any other unfortunate creature it lit upon. This was the Nucker who, though credited with flight, seems by his habitat in an icy and allegedly bottomless pool, more likely to have been a flightless water serpent, more prone to slithering and sliding across the ground than swooping and sailing through the air. The suggestion that he was a water creature is further supported by the fact that the Old English word 'nicor' means 'water monster' or 'water demon.' But if there is some uncertainty about his physical characteristics, let there be none about the havoc he wreaked around Lymington when he emerged form the dark depths of the Nucker Hole.

Now, by way of a brief interruption to the narrative, just a word about this 'bottomless pool': it remains there in Lymington today. Its depth is estimated at all of thirty feet. To continue . . .

The King of Sussex – rather a grand title for such rackety times - unable to do anything to protect his people, called out desperately for a hero to rid him and his lands of the terror, offering the reward of his daughter's hand in marriage in return. This is the stuff of legend, of fairy tale, of Hollywood western and (not unexpectedly) into the breech stepped a local lad. As ever the oral tradition rather blurs the plot. Some have it that a wandering knight turned up, slew the Nucker and married the princess. This version of the tale cries out for 'and lived happily ever after.'

A second version introduces Jim Puttock, a Lymington boy who, endowed with rustic cunning, prepared a huge suet pudding which he offered to the monster. Having swallowed the pudding too hurriedly the Nucker was

overcome with indigestion and Jim, taking
advantage of the beast's indisposition, cut off
its head with an axe.

A similar account credits a group of locals
with the killing of the Nucker after deciding in
desperation to take matters into their own
hands. They also produced a pudding and
held it out to the 'green, greasy and scaly'
beast at the end of a pole. The Nucker swallowed it all with one gulp. But the
pole was what really did for the monster, for it stuck in his gullet and, while
he writhed about, choking helplessly, the locals set about finishing him off,
cutting him up in small pieces.

And then there was Jim Pulk, another young fellow from the village, who
baked a huge pie which he laced with poison. He took it on a cart to the
Nucker Hole and left it there on the edge of the water. As always in these
stories, the Nucker came out and scoffed the lot and then died. Jim cut off its
head with his scythe and went to the Six Bells for a celebratory drink. But all
did not end well for Jim. He had carelessly left some of the poison on his
hands, and the inevitable happened.

Perhaps most of our medieval ancestors really believed that some time in
the past this had really occurred. It is difficult to estimate what proportion of
them was so gullible in the early seventeenth century, but the authors who
concocted the following fiction, must have been of the view that some of
their contemporaries would have no doubt of its veracity. It is extravagantly
titled 'A Discourse relating a strange and monstrous Serpent (or Dragon) lately
discovered, and yet living, to the great Annoyance and divers Slaughters both
of Men and Cattell, by his strong and violent Poyson: in Sussex, two miles
from Horsam, in a Woode called St Leonards Forest, and thirtie miles from
London, this present month of August, 1614.'

It continues:

'In Sussex, there is a pretty market towne, called Horsam, and neare unto
it a forrest, called St Leonard's Forrest, and there is an unfrequented place,
heathie, vaultie, full of unwholesome shades, and overgrowne hollowes, where
this serpent is thought to be bred; but, wheresoever bred, certaine and too
true it is, that there it yet lives. Within three or four miles compasse are its
usual haunts, oftentimes at a place called Faygate, and it hath been seene within

half a mile of Horsam; a wonder no doubte, most terrible and noisome to the inhabitants thereabouts. There is always in his track or path left a glutinous and slimie matter (as by a small similitude we may perceive in a snail's) which is very corrupt and offensive to the scent.

'This serpent (or dragon, as some call it) is reputed to be nine feete, or rather more, in length, and shaped almost in the forme of an axletree of a cart; a quantitie of thickness in the middest, and somewhat smaller at both endes. The former part, which he shootes forth as a necke, is supposed to be an elle long [four feet]; with a white ring, as it were, of scales about it. The scales along his backe seem to be blackish, and so much as is discovered under his bellie, appeareth to be red; for I speak of no nearer description than of a reasonable ocular distance. For coming too neare it, hath already been too dearly paid for, as you shall heare hereafter.

'It is likewise discovered to have large feete, but the eye may be there deceived; for some suppose that serpents have no feete. He is of countenance very proud, and at the sight or hearing of men or cattel, will raise his neck upright, and seem to listen and looke about, with great arrogancy. There are likewise upon either side of him discovered, two great bunches so big as a large foote-ball, and (as some thinke) will in time grow to wings; but God, I hope, will (to defend the poor people in the neighbourhood) that he shall be destroyed before he grow so fledge.

'He will cast his venome about four rodde [20 yards] from him, as by woefull experience it was proved on the bodies of a man and woman coming that way, who afterwards were found dead, being poysoned and very much swelled, but not prayed upon. Likewise a man going to chase it and, as he imagined, to destroy it with two mastive dogs, as yet not knowing the great danger of it, his dogs were both killed, and he himselfe glad to return with haste to preserve his own life. Yet this is to be noted, that the dogs were not prayed upon, but slaine and left whole; for his food is thought to be, for the most part, in a conie-warren, which he much frequents; and it is found much scanted and impaired in the increase it had wont to afford.

'The persons, whose names are hereunder printed, have seene this serpent, besides divers others, as the carrier of Horsam, who lieth at the White Horse in Southwark, and who can certifie the truth of all that has been here related.
John Steele, Christopher Holder and
a Widow Woman dwelling near Faygate.'

Was this an honest mistake? Were those who signed the document really convinced of the dragon's existence? Had a large serpent escaped from someone's private menagerie? Was it perhaps some kind of hoax? Was the real intention to keep people away from the Forest so that they would not interfere with the activities of smugglers? Was it a story put about to deter poachers? Take your pick.

What is perhaps more interesting is that the story suggests the kinds of imagined monsters that peopled the minds of ordinary folk in the seventeenth century. Mark Antony Lower, writing in the nineteenth century, said that his contemporaries still believed the Forest to be the haunt of monstrous snakes. Perhaps this story boosted earlier beliefs so that they lasted for at least two more centuries.

If in the nineteenth century people still believed that there were such beasts roaming St Leonard's Forest, they must also have been quite ready to accept the existence of Mrs Latham's 'oudacious large one' along with so many other curious beliefs.

The Poor Man

The Devil of legend, bumbler that he was, certainly clodhopped all over Sussex. Remarkable really that when he had so much of the world to look after, as well as a netherworld with screeching souls turning on spits for all eternity, there was still time for his cloven hoofs to dance all round the county. And odd for such an important personage to make such a fiasco of his efforts. Yet, for all his failures, he left his name all over the place.

For instance, there's Devil's Brook near Mount Caburn and the Devil's Ditch, a six mile long earthwork in West Sussex; there's the Devil's Bog in the Ashdown Forest and several fields across East and West Sussex are named Devil's Race. At Ditchling are the Devil's Humps, while his Jumps are near Treyford Hill and at Seaford we find Devil's Rest Bottom.

And then near Brighton is the Devil's Dyke, not so much the masterwork he intended but rather the indicator of his greatest flop. He had intended to drive a great wedge through the Downs so that the sea would rush through and flood the Weald. Cottages, farms, hamlets, villages and towns would be wiped out and all the people and animals living in them. But the wicked old fellow was well known for his tricks in this part of the world. The Poor Man, or He, or the Black Man, or Old Nick, Old Scratch, Old Grim, Old Man or Old Harry – or whatever name you may wish to call him by – had been around too long for people to fall for his mischief. On this occasion, he set about his work after dusk fell, intending that it should be finished by sunrise, for he could not stand sunlight. But by then he hoped to be away, lurking in the shadows while the floodwaters poured through the gap he had created. So he worked away heaving out great mounds of earth and creating what in time would come to be called Chanctonbury and Cissbury Rings, Rackham Hill, Mount Caburn and the Isle of Wight.

But before the last vital pieces of earth were removed the Devil was spotted. In the middle of a pitch black night, an old woman living in a cottage nearby heard him going about his work. And despite the darkened world, she recognised him, tall, thin, shadowless, his back hunched from endless carrying of sackloads of people off to Hell. She knew him all right and she knew what to do. She found the sieve that she used in her garden and held it up, placing behind it a lit candle. And that did the trick. Looking up, pausing in his work, the Devil saw this great shining orb. The sun, he thought to himself – and, picking up his tools in great haste, he was off as fast as he could, leaving the work unfinished. Nor did he ever come back to complete it.

And if an old woman with a candle and a sieve could best the Devil, what chance did he have against the blacksmith, St Dunstan of Mayfield? Turning up in the forge, disguised as a beautiful woman, failed to work. The skirt was too short and the cloven hoofs all to plain to see. The saint seized the Devil by the nose with his red hot pincers. Promises were exacted of future good behaviour, although naturally the Devil's word could never be trusted.

On another occasion Dunstan again outwitted the Devil, who on yet another night was intending some further dreadful catastrophe for Sussex. This time Dunstan alerted all the farmyard cocks in the Weald and made them crow. Fearing it was daylight, the Devil made off, another piece of work unfinished. Yet again Dunstan saved Mayfield by putting some of the horseshoes he had made on all of the houses. The Devil had never been able to stand up to the power of iron.

One story has it that the light from the old lady's candle and sieve actually killed the Devil and that he was buried in a nearby earthwork called the Devil's Grave. Next to it is the Devil's Wife's Grave. And, so they say, should you run round the Devil's Grave seven times – yes, the magical number seven – he will appear. There are other spots, too, should you wish to raise the Devil. For instance, walk round the Devil's Humps, the four large prehistoric barrows at Stoughton, and he will turn up. Or run seven times round Chanctonbury Ring and he will reward you with a bowl of soup or milk. There are other Devil-summoning sites at the Devil's Humps at Ditchling and at Mount Caburn, too.

But beware. This business of raising the Devil is fraught with danger, for once before you he is not easy to be rid of. Take care, for he may steal your soul away. Boys Firmin tells the story of a man who was said to have raised the Devil at Crowborough. Having managed the first part of the exercise, he found himself in the desperate situation of being unable to return him whence he came. Fortunately he had a quick-witted son who threw a sack of clover seeds on the ground. The Devil set about picking them up, but the son goaded him, jeered at him, telling him that he was far too clumsy, far too slow. The result was that the Devil, thoroughly humiliated, slunk away. Which only goes to prove yet again that Old Nick was not as clever as he thought himself to be.

Mighty though the Devil was thought to be, broad though his dominion, his failures at the hands of ordinary people are remarkable and he ends up not as a conqueror but rather as one who plays rather spiteful little tricks. For instance, there was a widespread belief that at sunrise on Easter Day the sun danced for joy. But this glorious sight was never seen because the Devil in his pettiness always put a hill in the way.

And he turned up at the most innocent of occasions. Country folk regularly gathered nuts in the autumn but it was said that 14 September was a particularly dangerous day to go nutting. It was the day when the wise would keep out of the woods. But for those who did go nutting on that day, he would be waiting, a tall man in black, his nutting bag in his hand, hiding his cloven feet as best he could, and he would be ever so courteous, holding down the branches so that the gatherers could reach the nuts more easily but all the while he would be ensnaring them and, said the warning, 'misfortune will follow them all through life'.

While some plants were said to deter the old fellow others were closely associated with him. There was Deadly Nightshade, most popularly called Devil's Herb, as the Devil had to go out at night to attend to it. Nettles in Sussex went by the name of the Devil's Playthings. He had wild flowers and weeds named after him: Devil's Guts (the parasitic dodder); the Devil's Churnstaff (sun spurge); and the Devil's Own Parsley (wild hedge parsley). He was, and is, all over the countryside.

And then there were the ripe, full-fruited blackberries along the hedgerows, always eagerly sought. But then along he would come once more with his mean little tricks, this time spitting on all the bushes and so signifying the end of the blackberry season. Charlotte Latham tells of a farmer's wife living in Arundel who used to make large quantities of blackberry jam. One day she realised that she had not picked enough and she asked one of her servants to send out her children to gather three or four pints more. The woman was horrified.

'Ma'am, don't you know this is the eleventh of October. Bless me, ma'am, and you ask me to let my children go out blackberrying! I thought everybody knew that the Devil went round on the tenth of October and spat on all the blackberries and that if any person were to eat one on the eleventh day they or someone belonging to them would die or fall into great trouble before the year was out. No, nothing should persuade me to let any child of mine go blackberrying on the eleventh of October.'

Naturally, there were stories of people who were said to have had personal contact with the Devil who walked among them. They had even made Faustian pacts with him and a number of court cases allegedly took place in the county involving those who carried a written document to the effect that they were in league with the Devil. The story goes that Mike Mills, a smuggler, raced the Devil through St Leonard's Forest, the wager being that should he win the Devil would leave his soul alone for ever. Mills won the race and the Devil lost a soul. Sadly, in the circumstances, Heaven would not accept the smuggler.

But even if these tales depict a Devil who is easily outwitted, precautions against his power were taken seriously for after all he was seen as a magic force. Even the churches were security conscious and kept firmly shut the doors in their north walls lest the Devil made entry there. There are these so-called Devil's Doors in churches at Sompting and Worth, Jevington and Birdham. The doors were opened during the baptism of children when the priest exorcised the spirit of the Devil which made off through the north door. In some churches the north wall doors were completely and permanently blocked.

In the eighteenth century there were people at Cuckfield who believed that the Devil lived among the tombstones in the churchyard, and there was a conviction that if he would only show himself by daylight he could be chased out of the parish for ever. But the old stealer of souls was never caught there.

Foolish and inept as the legends portrayed the Devil, many in times past believed that he really did stalk the fields and lanes promoting mischief, that he was everywhere waiting to ensnare the careless.

In 1645 after two disastrous years as county gaoler at Horsham, the former shoemaker, Richard Luckins, was charged with various misdemeanours. His behaviour had been scandalous: he was constantly fighting, blaspheming, drinking heavily and ill-treating his prisoners. One of the charges against him states that, after the escape of a man named Southwood and several others, Luckins 'sent a servant of his to persons suspected of witchcrafte and them that Deale in such Diabolicall [things] to bring back Southwood and others his prisoners again. Luckins himself saying in the presence of Divers [others] that he would make use of the devil.' Luckins ended up a prisoner in his own gaol, guilty it seems of incompetence and corruption rather than attempting to consort with the Devil. Lucky Luckins!

Within a hundred years, at least on the face of it, the Devil's position had altered. Though the clergy had always painted a dark picture of the Devil, in folklore he seems to have been an almost naive and useless figure doing little more than spitting on blackberries and trying unsuccessfully to flood the Weald. By the time of the 1736 Witchcraft Act, however, it was no longer illegal to engage in witchcraft for it was no longer thought to exist. And along with the rejection of the dark arts went a belief in the Devil. At least, that is what the lawmakers and the philosophers thought. Anyone claiming to cast spells or carry out any of the traditional tasks of the witch was simply a fraud and would be charged accordingly. But such enlightened beliefs were not shared by the vast majority of the population whose faith in the power of the Devil and his magic was undiminished.

Just be on the alert, they told themselves. Take care. He is the great tempter. And don't forget the poacher up at Northchapel. Got drunk one night, wouldn't leave the local inn. 'May the Devil burn me if I do,' he was shouting at the innkeeper and others present. Next day they found a great pile of ash and the stink of brimstone. Don't invite him to do anything. He may take you at our word!

So put up the usual charms about the house and barn. Maybe hang charms on your animals for he goes after the beasts of the field. He can mark them, destroy them. Remember his fingerprints are on the foreleg of every pig. Horse brasses, nice and shiny, they'll keep him away. Put a couple of crossed scythes on your haystacks. Stick a sprig of hellebore in the pig's ear. Always keep a ha'penny or some small change about you, in your pocket or your purse, maybe in a cash box. If you don't he'll be there, ferreting about, making mischief and you'll never have money again. He will forever be urging you to commit evil and then you will be his forever for he will take your soul. And don't do silly things like cutting your nails on a Sunday: if you do he'll chase you for the rest of your days. Just a few precautions to bear in mind. Those lawyers and people in parliament think they've done away with him, but they haven't.

Demonic possession? We hear of it in 1743 when John Breads of Rye appeared in court for the murder of Alan Grebell, a local magistrate, a crime for which he was executed. During the trial Breads claimed to have been driven by 'a parcel of devils' on a previous occasion when he had attacked 'William Foul in a lane, called Dead Man's Lane, just without the town'.

And thirty years later, despite the law which decriminalised witchcraft, references to the Devil being the initiator of crime were still not expunged from legal documents. Take the 1776 indictment of Ann Cruttenden at Horsham Assizes which stated:

'The Jurors for our Lord the King upon their Oath Present That Ann the wife of Joseph Cruttenden late of the Parish of Brightling in the County of Sussex Butcher not having the fear of God before her eyes but being moved and seduced by the instigation of the Devil on the fifteenth day of June in the Sixteenth year of the reign of our Sovereign Lord George the third now King of Great Britain & with force and Arms at the Parish aforesaid in the County aforesaid in and upon the said Joseph Cruttenden her husband in the peace of God and our said Lord the King then and there being feloniously treacherously wilfully and of her malice aforethought did make an Assault . . .'

Note those words, from another age: 'moved and seduced by the instigation of the Devil'.

Ann Cruttenden, by the way, had stabbed her husband of eight years in the throat. He was 43 years of age and she was 80. Found guilty of murder, she was sentenced 'to be Drawn on a Hurdle and Burned with fire until she be dead'. Accordingly, the sentence was carried out.

But the real point here is that the Devil still had not yet quit the stage. In 1831 John Holloway, Brighton's first trunk murderer, strangled his wife, Celia, in Donkey Row in the presence of his mistress, Ann Kennett. But once the murder was done Holloway was bewildered. What about the body? What should he do with it? At first he hadn't the courage to dismember it. In his confession Holloway said, 'I did not know what to do with her. I was not able to carry her away. I attempted to cut [dismember] her but I had not the heart till the Devil himself, with all his united powers [told me what to do].' He was not blaming the Devil for the murder. Rather he was suggesting that it was the Devil's quick wittedness which gave him the courage to complete his awful work.

In the course of the trial the heavily pregnant Ann Kennett frequently interrupted her former lover. 'Whenever he introduced her name at critical periods of the dreadful tale, she threw herself into paroxysms of rage, and loaded him with execrations.' As she dissociated herself from the crime, 'The Devil's at your elbow,' and 'the Devil's in your eyes,' were expressions which she called out in court to her former lover.

No, the Devil had not been totally abandoned. Nor had he abandoned the people of Sussex.

In 1867 Alfred Gibbons, son of the postmaster at Hurst Green, appeared in court for the theft of money from letters in his father's office. He claimed that the Devil tempted him. No, young Gibbons is saying, it is not social conditions to blame for my fall from grace; it is not living in squalor in an impoverished home; it is the Devil. He is responsible.

Emily Coram, a 39 year-old, admitted to the Lewes Road Hospital for Women and Children in 1905 after a nervous breakdown, slit the throat of a baby, Louis Cooke, with a penknife. She then confessed what she had done to the matron.

'Satan, the Devil, tempted me,' she said. 'I thought if I did something dreadful in this world it would be easier for me in the next. The Devil told me to kill the child: I know I am lost. I have only found out lately that I am not a Christian. I feel voices inside telling me I am lost and they made me do it. A voice asked me, When were you converted? Satan said to me, Your punishment will be less in eternity for the sins you have committed if you do something desperate.'

Emily was found guilty but insane, as was John Jordan five years later. The 39 year old soldier was charged with the murder of a child at Climping Fort. He had been reported for being absent overnight by Bombardier Semple with the result that Jordan was not granted permission to transfer to Dover where his wife lived. In revenge, Jordan cut young Semple's throat and 'did not deny the fact but said the Devil must have tempted him to do it'.

The Devil is named in many a courtroom over the years, in cases similar to the above. This was not the fumbling goat-footed dolt who failed to flood the Weald, nor was he any longer outwitted by old country women with sieves. No more was he in the background, leaving the witch centre-stage. Here, before judge and jury, he was authoritative, a being of power, present at the side of the wicked, whispering to them, urging them.

It was as though he was reminding the world that he was still here, a mighty presence, still working, never yet banished by so-called 'reason' and the petty laws of mankind.

Not that the courts accepted claims of demonic possession. These, they dismissed as some kind of figure of speech or as delusional or most frequently as downright dishonest. The Devil had and has no status in law which does leave us with something of a conundrum, for the Church, through a deeply religious rite, continues to exorcise him from the possessed.

The Devil, then – fact or fiction? A figure of superstition? Or not?

'The Pharisees'

There is such a confusion about fairies, what they looked like, what they did, whether they were kindly or troublesome. It is likely that the confusion was always there, back in the days when so many people believed in their existence. All that remains today are the places they were thought to frequent, a tenuous folk-memory, traces of an old name. All of those sites with Pook or Puck in their name are where our forefathers located them, the Old English word 'puca' meaning imp, goblin or fairy.

So to Rusper and Pook's Hill or Puck Stye Farm at Hartfield or the now lost Pook Ryde at Cuckfield. There are farms and copses and closes throughout East and West Sussex with names such as Pook Hole, Pook Croft, Pook Bourne. There is Pook Lane near Chichester and Pookchurch Wood near Handcross. And at Selmeston there was in William Parish's time an allegedly haunted cottage, Pook Hale (Hall).

If you find these are not evidence enough of our ancestors' belief in fairies, you may find it difficult to accept as fact that Harrow Hill near Worthing was the last home of the fairies in England and that their burial ground was at The Mount at Pulborough. Some will quibble over these locations: some will subscribe to the view that the fairies' last resort was in the flint mines at Patching. But there was a general acceptance that they danced regularly at Cissbury Ring and at Park Mound as well as on Chanctonbury Ring, particularly on Midsummer Eves.

But is there any evidence of their ever having been seen? And please don't sneer at the unsophisticated views of the past. Though they displayed as much or as little sense as we do, our Sussex forebears were neither well travelled nor decently educated. Take the case of the man who went to London for the first time and who commented on his return, 'What a queer large place! Why, it ain't like Newick and it ain't like Chailey!'

The poet and artist, William Blake, who lived at Felpham from 1800 to 1803, swore that he had seen a fairy funeral. 'I was walking alone in my garden,' he said. 'There was a great stillness among the branches and flowers,

104

and more than a common sweetness in the air. I heard a low and pleasant sound and I knew not whence it came. At last I saw the broad leaf of a flower move, and underneath I saw a procession of creatures, of the size and colour of green and grey grasshoppers, bearing a body laid out on a rose leaf, which they buried with songs and then disappeared. It was a fairy's funeral.' And the figures are not unlike the dancing fairies in his painting, 'Oberon, Titania and Puck'. There is no indication of what kind of medication Blake might have been on at the time of this alleged funeral.

But was it evidence? Not quite, because the poet's view is not in accordance with that given by a witness at Steyning a hundred years later. He claimed to have seen 'a little brown pointy-eared person who lay under the shadow of a gorse bush, not ten feet away. His chin was propped on his hands, his legs were kicking behind him, and he was grinning from ear to ear under the shadow of the tall pointed greeny-brown cap. He was there one minute and gone the next.'

How like the images of some of the fairy folk who appeared in our long-gone children's picture books.

In Janet Bord's book, *Fairies: Real Encounters with Little People*, published in 1997, she records a witness as having seen 'a small hairy man . . . no more than eighteen inches high and covered in hair. His face was bare but had a leathery look.' Now that is more in keeping with how long-dead Sussex countrymen were describing fairies, more in keeping with Kipling's Puck who condemned those 'little buzzflies with butterfly wings and gauze petticoats and shiny stars in their hair and a wand like a schoolteacher's cane for punishing bad boys and rewarding good ones!'

A couple of hundred years ago a Sussex man explained that 'a pharisee was a little creature rather bigger than a squirrel and not quite so large as a fox'. And parenthetically, just to clear up the word 'pharisee': there was some confusion in past times – and not just in Sussex, by the way – about this corrupted plural of 'fairy', the result perhaps of too much sitting in church or chapel and too little paying attention to what was being said.

Not that a belief in fairies was necessarily universal in the old days. From the eighteenth century onwards there were growing doubts about all of these ancient beliefs. A farm labourer at Burlough Castle in Milton Street had heard a fairy muttering to himself 'I've been a-bakin' and I've broken my peel [baker's shovel].' The labourer picked up the peel and repaired it. But when he told the parish clerk what had happened, the story was abruptly dismissed. He was told that 'it was all a galushion [illusion] and dere wan't no pharisees nowadays.'

But the fairy rings so clearly marked in the grass? What about them? Wasn't that where the fairies danced at night? Certainly nobody in past times would have come up with the idea of their being a kind of fungus. Mark Antony Lower, the Sussex antiquarian, recounts a story by someone he calls 'Fowington', presumably an inhabitant of Folkington.

'Besides, though I have never seen any of 'em, my grandmother, who was a very truthful woman, has, time and again. They was liddle folks not more than a foot high, and used to be uncommon fond of dancing. They joined hands and formed a circle and danced upon it till the grass came three times greener there as it was anywheres else. That's how these here rings come upon the hills. Leastways so they say, but I don't know nothing about it intire [entirely] for I never seen none an' 'em. Besides, there's an old song that we always sing at harvest supper, where it comes in "We'll drink and dance like pharisees". Now, I should like to know why it's put like that 'ere in the song, if it ain't true.'

No doubt about it. 'Fowington' was convinced by his grandmother's words.

It was said that the fairies could be summoned 'on a moonlight night just when the pollen was ripe on the catkins'. You just had to go to one of the usual enchanted locations, taking with you two small catkin branches. You waved then gently and sang:

Come in the stillness,
Come in the night,
Come soon, and bring delight.
Beckoning, beckoning,
Left hand and right,
Come now, Ah, come tonight.

Alternatively, in the absence of catkins, you could run nine times round a fairy ring. Either way you would hear music and laughter from their underground home and then out they'd come. You would think that with that kind of story going the rounds, what with people singing verses, waving catkins and running round in circles, the fairies would never get a wink of sleep.

Sometimes there was a degree of kindness in the fairies' dealings with people. They were said to reward hard-working servant girls by putting a small silver coin into their shoes. The cynical might think this to be more likely a trick by employers to get even more work out of their employees. After all, a coin from an employer was fine, but it could not compare with one from a fairy.

And fairies were often most helpful to farmers. Charlotte Latham tells a story which illustrates how helpful they could be. Once upon a time – which seems a not inappropriate beginning – two men stole a farmer's pig and put it in a sack. They stopped for a moment and by chance laid the sack just over a hole where a fairy lived. Knowing what they had done the fairy climbed into the sack in place of the pig. The men took it in turns to carry the sack but it now seemed so very heavy. Then the man carrying the sack suddenly noticed a little figure running by his side and calling out, 'Dick, Dick, where be you?' Then a voice from the sack replied:

In a sack,
Pick-a-back,
Riding up Beeding Hill.

In horror the thief threw down the sack and he and his companion ran away, at which point the good fairy resumed his own form and returned home, happy to have saved the farmer's pig.

The fairies were thought to help around the house and in the barn and dairy. When the butter was slow in forming Mrs Latham often heard her cook repeating:

Come, butter, come,
Come, butter, come,
Peter stands at the gate,
Waiting for a buttered cake,
Come, butter, come.

This charm was repeated three times to make any witch responsible beat a retreat and bring in the helpful Master Dobbs, a house fairy or brownie who did all sorts of housework. J.K. Rowling has a household elf called Dobby in several of her books. This is probably a nod in the direction of Master Dobbs, In East Sussex, in particular, 'Master Dobbs must've been helping you' was a common expression to use to a person who had done more work than was expected.

But helpful or not, Master Dobbs seems to have had the same character defect that many of his fellows suffered from. Apparently he always wore a rather tattered hat. One night a grateful farmer brought him a new one, but instead of expressing gratitude Dobbs turned on the farmer angrily. 'A new hat, a new hat!' he yelled, and then, referring to himself in the third person, he went on, 'Dobbs will do no more good!' He never returned to that farm. Presumably he was insulted. Rather a thin-skinned gang then, some of these fairies.

It was said that fairies would always work hard for people who treated them with respect, but let there be the slightest slip – no matter how unwitting – and they would flounce out. Offer them a bowl of milk and they were satisfied, but offer them a new suit of clothes and they would be deeply offended. And then they could turn very unpleasant, obstructing work and being deliberately destructive. Another rule seems to be that no mortal ever addressed them.

Here is Lower again in 1854, writing on this very matter, this time with the story of how 'an ol' brother of my wife's gurt gran'mother see some pharisees once, and 'twould a been a power better if so be he hadn't never seen 'em, or leastways never offended 'em.' Jeems Meppom, described as 'a liddle farmer', usually did his own threshing. One season he suddenly discovered that when he went back to the barn each morning great quantities of his corn had been threshed. Someone must be doing his work for him in the night, and this puzzled him but being 'an out-and-out bold chep, dat didn't fear man nor devil, as de sayin' is, he made up his mind dat he'd goo over some night to see how 'twas managed.'

One night Jeems hid in the barn and about midnight he saw 'a couple of liddle cheps about eighteen inches high or dereaway come into de barn without uppening the doors.' He watched while they took off their jackets and set about the threshing. Finally they had a rest and Jeems heard one of them say to his companion in a squeaky voice, 'I say, Puck, I twet [sweat]. Do you twet?' At this point Jeems just could not help laughing out loud. But the fairies were so offended that they picked up their flails ready to leave 'and as dey passed him he felt sich a queer pain in his head as if somebody had gi'en him a lamentable hard thump wud a hammer, dat knocked him down as flat as a flounder.'

The doctor was called to his home but Jeems had little faith in him: 'De cuss of the pharisees is uppon me, and all de stuff in your shop can't do me no good.' And Mas' Meppom was right, for about a year ahtewuds [afterwards] he died, poor man, sorry enough dat he'd ever interfered wud things dat didn't consarn him.'

William Parish, vicar of Selmeston and another great nineteenth century recorder of Sussex life, gives another version of the story which he heard from a local farmer:

'I've heard my father say that when he lived over the hill there was a carter that worked on the farm along wid him, and no one couldn't think how 'twas that this here man's horses looked so much better than what any one else's did. I've heard my father say that they was that fat that they couldn't scarcely get about; and this here carter, he was just as much puzzled as what the rest was, so cardinley [accordingly] he laid hisself up in the stable one night to find if he could find the meaning on't.

'And he hadn't been there very long before these here liddle pharisees, they crep in at the sink hole; in they crep, one after another, liddle tiny bits of chaps they was, and each an 'em had a little sack of corn on his back as much as ever he could carry. Well, in they crep, on they gets, up they clims, and there they was, just as busy feeding these here horses; and prensley one says to t'other, "Puck," says he, "I twets. Do you twet?" And thereupon, this here carter he jumps up and says, "Dannel ye," he says, "I'll make ye twet afore I've done wud ye!" But afore he could get anigh 'em they was all gone; every one an 'em.

'And I've heard my father say that from that day forard this here carter's horses fell away, till they got that thin and poor that he couldn't a-bear to be seen along wid 'em, so he took and went away, for he couldn't a-bear to see hisself no longer, and nobody ain't seen him since.'

The fairies were certainly not like those we read about in our childhood books. No diaphanous dresses, no wings, no wands, nothing of that kind. These Sussex fairies were an altogether different breed and feared rather than loved by some people. For example, a clergyman, hoping to improve the educational standards of young people in his parish, started an evening school. He challenged the mother of one of the boys who failed to attend. She explained that her son was afraid that he would meet the 'pharisees' at night. He was, his mother said, using a good old Southern English word to describe it, 'that timmersome that he couldn't a-bear to go out after dark'.

Not such agreeable little fellows as we might have thought then, these fairies.

Bits and pieces

Concerning beginnings, nothing new should be started on a Friday - for example a journey, a new job, and a marriage. Not even the writing of a book should be started on that day. Charles Igglesden, writing in the 1930s, asserted that there were fewer burglaries on Fridays because of burglars' anxieties about how things might turn  out. This suspicion that we have about Friday may be related to its being at the end of the week, a day no longer fresh, a day stained by sweat, a day worn out by the labour of the other working days. Generally we set about a New Year, a new season, a new week with some hope for the future. But not on a Friday.

A peacock's tail feathers should not be allowed inside the house as they bear the emblem of the evil eye.

If you should drop your umbrella, let someone else pick it up and you'll have a nice surprise.

And just as fishermen always move their boats 'sunwise' (clockwise), there are curious observances on land about laying the table 'sunwise'; about passing the port; about stirring the cake mix and the tea pot.

It's good luck if you find a piece of coal and take it into the house. At least, so they say. Perhaps it would be wise to touch wood.

Give away as much parsley as you like, provided that you do not give away the root. An old gardener, usually so generous with his help to others, had refused to give away his parsley for transplant. Asked why this should be, he answered that if he did so he would lose his job within the year. That was what had happened to two gardeners he had known. Both 'changed masters in the year'.

This is a cardinal rule: you must show respect to the new moon. So bow or curtsy when you see it. Never in any circumstances point at it – that's very discourteous.

Some charms are come upon quite by chance. Pebbles with a hole through the centre, often picked up on beaches, were thought to be especially lucky, and not only by fishermen. Not only were they used as protective charms in houses and barns, but children played with them.

They used to throw the stone over the left shoulder and chant:

Lucky stone, lucky, go over my head,
And bring me some luck before I go to bed.

Go out stick gathering in the woods on a Sunday and the Man in the Moon will come down and carry you off.

It's bad luck if you open an umbrella indoors or pick up your own glove if you have dropped it.

Put on your right shoe first. There are all sorts of warnings about the left not being right! It used to be thought that after you spilt salt, you should throw some over your left shoulder to blind the Devil who was lurking there. The Latin word for 'left' is 'sinister', a word we have taken into the language to describe someone or something which is dangerous or untrustworthy.

Sing before breakfast, you'll cry before night. Just a reminder to you that life isn't always easy. Don't go thinking it is or you'll come a cropper. That is one of the central themes of superstition.

There is a long-established general dislike of doing domestic work on New Year's Day. In a letter to *The Times* of May 22, 1934, a correspondent from Singleton wrote that if any clothes were washed that day, the life of a family member would be washed away.

If you catch a falling leaf you will have good luck for the rest of the year.

If you have new clothes make sure that you wear them first on a Sunday, better still at church. In this way they will be blessed and they will last longer. In *Field and Hedgerow*, published in 1889. Richard Jefferies has a cautionary tale. He says that if you wear any new article of clothing for the first time on a Saturday, you must expect to be severely punished. A man of his acquaintance had put on a pair of new boots on a Saturday and on the following Monday he broke his arm

Crossed knives or a crossed knife and fork could mean a forthcoming quarrel or even death. This is strange because the sign of the cross is good and protective and so is metal. Perhaps it has something to do with crossed swords in a battle.

It is lucky if you accidentally put on your stocking inside out but when you discover your mistake don't try to correct it. That will bring bad luck.

A correspondent from Kingston, East Sussex, to the *Observer* in 1927 writes: 'While I do not think that there is any definite evidence that mushrooms only grow when the moon is growing, it is a very widespread belief among country folk in general. Many rustic gardeners never plant seeds except during this period even today.'

If you find nine peas in the first pod you shell, you will have good luck.

There is a number of superstitions about moving house. In 1984 a lady from Rogate remarked: 'When you move, you have to leave some salt behind in the old house – just a little bit. Funny, isn't it?'

William Parish referred to 'January butter', by which he meant 'mud.' It was considered lucky to bring mud into the house in this month, presumably because it meant that someone was employed.

You must not turn a feather bed on a Sunday or the person who sleeps on it will have fearful dreams for the rest of the week. As they used to say, he would be 'hag-ridden' – that is, as if he were being ridden by a witch. Witches traditionally rode horses from stables in the night. And now we have the word 'nightmare.'

It is lucky to be the first in the house to open the door on Christmas morning and to call out, 'Welcome, old Father Christmas!'

'Now, as custom is,' read a letter to the *Brighton Gazette* in 1887, 'off went our bonnets to a chimney sweep, sitting cross-legged, tailor-wise, on the rough plank of a shabby pony cart. It is said to bring luck, this bowing to a black man.'

Always cut your hair and your nails and kill your pig at the waxing of the moon.

A witch on trial in Sussex in the nineteenth century was described as 'most unlike our old ideal image of a witch, being a remarkably tall, fat, rosy, good tempered looking woman.' It's a comment that might easily be made today.

Midsummer's Eve was the evening when witches, fairies and ghosts were said to be out and about. At Broadwater there was an old oak tree in a north east corner of the green. Here a group of skeletons was said to rise up and dance round the tree to the rhythm of their rattling bones.

Your feet itching? You'll tread new ground. Itching elbow? Expect a fresh bedmate. On the right hand? Look out for some money. The left hand? Look out for a stranger or a kiss or a curse. A tingling in your right ear? Someone is saying some very nice things about you. And a tingling in your left ear? What do you expect? Someone is speaking ill of you.

Make a wish when you see a piebald pony and when you eat the first fruit of the season.

Seeing the new moon through glass results in bad luck. One housemaid always shut her eyes when closing the curtains at the time of the new moon. It is also unlucky to see it through the boughs of a tree. Break the evil influence by taking a coin out of your pocket and spitting on each side of it. In fact if you turn your silver coins over in your pocket at the time of the new moon it will double itself.

Small white specks on your fingernails are believed to be significant. These specks are called 'gifts':

A gift on the thumb
Is sure to come;
A gift on the finger
Is sure to linger.

William Parish says that the market women used to spit on the first coin from the first sale of the day. Then they would put it in a pocket by itself for luck.

It is said that the ground where human blood has been shed is cursed and will remain barren for ever. The once lush grass in a field at Kirdford withered away after a poacher was shot.

A notoriously bad character living by himself in a lonely place at the foot of the Downs was said to be nightly haunted by evil spirits in the form of rats. He could be heard cursing them and asking them to let him rest in peace. One old woman said that they were sent as a judgement on him and that some night they would carry him away. Despite this forecast, he was killed in a pub brawl.

Put your shoes on the table and there is a variety of possible bad outcomes ranging from a quarrel to imminent death. You could try spitting on the shoes as an antidote.

Conclusion

In the preceding pages I have indicated that profoundly felt superstitious belief began its long decline about 400 years ago. I have described some of these old superstitions, although I must admit that I have drawn on only a minority of them. There are more to unearth, and I believe that to be a worthwhile task for someone else, for it will take us nearer to the people of the past and deepen our understanding  of how they interpreted the world in which they found themselves. I hope that here I have at least drawn together the tangled and broken threads of some of the superstitions of Sussex – the first attempt to do so, I believe, since Charlotte Latham's work in 1878.

I think that I now know the kinds of interpretations my great-grandmother, born in 1850, must have made about the place she lived in and the things that happened to her and the people she knew. I wonder: did she believe in fairies? Did she believe in spells cast by malevolent witches? Did she try to conjure up the wraith of her future husband? Even if she personally did not do so, she must have known, living when she did, some who still held on with conviction to those older ideas and rituals, which the Enlightenment had not scrubbed away. It is staggering to think that some of her world view owed something to the medieval period or to some even older time.

Not that my great-grandmother would believe in dragons. They had disappeared from the public imagination a couple of centuries or more before she was born. But I'm confident that she would have known some of the fishermen of her small home town by the sea and would not have queried their seriously observed superstitions.

But today we are different, a sceptical, hard-nosed people, not the sort of people who you would think would fall for any of this old-fashioned nonsense. And yet, as I said in the introduction, I listened to a young man on a train quite recently who fancied that a pair of socks worn on match days determined the fortunes of his favourite football team. And I related the story of my neighbour who believes the outcome of the lottery draw in some strange way depends upon him. Can we really wonder at the people of the past when our own minds are still littered with notions of this nature?

Of course, the truth is that for the most part our superstitions now are milk-and water-stuff, rather vague in their promises of unspecified good luck or their threats of ill fortune. These are so often empty tokens, absolutely meaningless, their origins obscure and misunderstood. The richness of past symbols and rituals has been diluted. The business about walking under ladders, saying 'rabbits' at the beginning of the month, wearing a particular suit for an interview – they are believed in only half-heartedly these days. But at one time they held some real significance.

Let us not forget these old beliefs. For good or ill, some of them shaped our forefathers' lives. Logical or not, they are part of the equation of our history.

Bibliography

Albery, William *A Millennium of Facts in the History of Horsham and Sussex*
Horsham Museum Society, 1947

Allen, Andrew *A Dictionary of Sussex Folk Medicine* Countryside Books, 1995

Anson, Peter *Fisher Folk-Lore* The Faith Press, 1965

Baines, J Manwaring *Historic Hastings* F.J. Parsons, 1963

Behague, John *Lucky Sussex* Pomegranate Press, 1998

Bord, Janet *Fairies: Real Encounters with Little People* Michael O'Mara, 1997

Candlin, Lillian *Memories of Old Sussex* Countryside Books, 1987

Crook, Diana (*ed*) A Lewes Diary [The diary of Mrs Henry Dudeney]
Tartarus press, 1998

Davies, Owen *Witchcraft, Magic and Culture 1736-1951*
Manchester University Press 1999

Egerton, John Coker *Sussex Folk and Sussex Ways* Chatto & Windus 1892;
reprinted by Country Books, 2004

Firmin, Boys *An Illustrated Guide to Crowborough*
Hansard Publishing Union, 1890

Geering, Thomas *Our Sussex Parish* Methuen, 1884; reprinted by Country
Books, 2003

Gordon, H.D. *A History of Harting* W. Davy, 1877

Gregory Albert H. *Mid-Sussex through the Ages* Charles Clarke, 1938

Hare, Augustus *The Years with Mother* Barnes, Malcolm (*ed*)
Century Publishing, 1984

Igglesden, Charles *Those Superstitions* Gale Research Co, 1974

Johnson, W.H. *A Grim Almanac of Sussex* The History Press, 2007

Johnson, WH *Early Victorian Alfriston* Downsway Books, 1993

Latham, Charlotte *Some West Sussex Superstitions Lingering in 1868–1878*
Folklore Record, 1878

Lovett, Edward *Folklore and Legend of the Surrey Hills and of the Sussex Downs and
Forests* Caterham Valley, 1928

Lucas, E.V. *Highways and Byways in Sussex* Macmillan, 1904

Monod, Paul Kleber *The Murder of Mr Grebell* Yale University Press, 2003

Opie, Iona and Tatem, Moira *A Dictionary of Superstitions* OUP, 1989

Parish, Rev William D, *A Dictionary of the Sussex Dialect*
  Farncombe & Co, Lewes, 1875; reprinted by Country Books, 2001 and
  Snake River Press, 2008
Roud, Steve *Penguin Guide to the Superstitions of Britain and Ireland* Penguin, 2003
Simpson, Jacqueline *The Folklore of Sussex* Tempus, 2002
Wales, Tony *The West Sussex Village Book* Countryside Books, 1999
Wales, Tony *A Sussex Garland* Geoffrey Cave Associates, 1979
Wells, Roger (ed) *Victorian Village: the Diaries of the Revd John Coker Egerton of
  Burwash 1857–1888* Alan Sutton, 1992

Some other sources:

Catching Stories: Voices from the Brighton Fishing Community
  QueenSpark Books, 1988
Folklore, the journal of the Folklore Society
Sussex Notes and Queries Sussex Archaeological Society
Hastings and St Leonards Observer
Sussex Advertiser
Sussex Agricultural Express
Sussex County Magazine Vols 1 -30, 1927–1956
West Sussex Gazette
Internet: *Schwa's Page* – Sussex Archaeology and Folklore